Beyond Beijing

The Next Step for Women

Beyond Beijing

The Next Step for Women

A Personal Journal

Joan Chittister

Sheed & Ward

Sheed & Ward™ is a service of The National Catholic Reporter Publishing Company.

Library of Congress Cataloguing-in-Publication Data

Chittister, Joan
    Beyond Beijing : the next step for women / Joan Chittister.
      p.   cm.
    ISBN 1-55612-903-3 (alk. paper)
    1. Women's rights. 2. UN World Conference on Women.
  3. Chittister, Joan--Journeys. 4. China--Description and travel.
  5. Former Soviet republics--Description and travel.   I. Title.
HQ1236.C48 1996
305.42--dc20   96-6966
                                                   CIP

Published by: Sheed & Ward
                    115 E. Armour Blvd.
                    P.O. Box 419492
                    Kansas City, MO 64141-6492

To order, call: (800) 333-7373

Contents

Dedication

*This book is dedicated to my mother
who modeled for me years ago
those qualities upon which
the liberation of women
rests today:
the strength to perdure,
the courage to persevere.*

Preface

I admit that I can't quite shake off the images. They lurk there in the back of my mind like cobwebs in a musty basement. "Me and Marco Polo," I keep saying to myself. Me and Marco Polo. The figure of this one white explorer in the middle of a China that had had little or no contact whatsoever with the West has always stirred a singular fascination in me. It isn't that I know much about him. I'm sure, in fact, that I never knew as much about him as teachers thought I should. Nevertheless, there was something in the openness, the fearlessness, the single-mindedness of such a figure that brought out a wandering heart in me in a way that nothing else seemed to touch in quite the same manner. The memories are still clear: Fourth-grade history class. Sister in black serge citing the importance to East-West relations of this voyage of a man obviously mad to have gone so far with so little clear promise of gain, such minimal resources, such slender security. This one man's accounts of his travels to China remained the predominant Western image of China, she said, until the late 19th century. Me and Marco Polo? Well, hardly. But the fact remains that I, too, am now on my way to the Orient, and what I see there and describe to others about what happens there may well affect people yet. Not to the same extent, of course, but with much the same consequences on the way women and men view one another now as that one person's experience years ago affected the way the West saw the East for years to come.

To me China is still a strange and inscrutable place, ancient, remote, suspicious, and closed to the West, maybe as much because of us as because of them. China is a world inside the world. It is a culture, a government, a religion unto itself. And it is about to be the site of the Fourth UN Conference on Women, that majority of the human race who are also a world within a world. They are separate from the men who run it, completely other to men who call themselves its norm, totally unlike but essentially the same as the men who, on the one hand, assume that their lives subsume the lives of women and, on the other hand, consider women the unknown and delightfully inferior species. Maybe

China, the culture that signals difference, is, at least for symbolic reasons, the best possible place in the world to have such a conference as this.

There are people in the West, however, who say that we should not be holding any international meeting of global importance in China, let alone the Fourth UN World Conference on Women. China's human rights record is at least in question, if not abysmal, they say. The country's "son preference," a euphemism for the female infanticide that has deep roots in China's history and is now unarguably renewed by the country's one-child policy, signals the negative value afforded to women there and makes it a strange place to extol the rights of women, they say. The totalitarianism of the place may even make it dangerous for us, we are told. I suppose that all of that is true – at least to some extent – but, on the other hand, that may be exactly the reason that we, women, should go there. There is absolutely nothing like walking into the lion's den to prove that lions don't scare you. One thing for sure: I am not afraid. In my mother's name, I am not afraid.

The Peace Train

I don't make it a habit to write about events, at least not until they're over and there's been a chance to reflect on what happened there and what it means to people in the real world. This event, I think, deserves different treatment. This one starts with people in the real world.

By the time this column goes to press, I will already be well on my way to Beijing. That is, frankly, not all that unusual. After all, there are, at last report, about 38,000 other women — a veritable small city of women, in fact — going to the Fourth UN International Conference on Women, as well. Taken on face value, the trip itself is not so unique. The United Nations — people everywhere now — hold international conventions every day. There have even been three other international conferences on women alone. What may well be unique about this trip, though, is the way it's being done.

At the invitation of Peacelinks, an organization based in Pittsburgh, I will be going to Beijing by Peace Train. The Peace Train will take 230 women from 42 nations of the world through nine countries from Helsinki to Beijing, stopping in each to hold discussions and seminars with women's groups along the way.

Is the undertaking a significant one? Think of it this way:

The distance from New York to Los Angeles is 2800 miles or about five days of driving time if you drive 10 hours a day at an average of 60 miles per hour. The distance from Helsinki to Beijing along this route is more than 6000 miles and will take 23 days of train travel to complete. Awesome. Maybe even grueling.

What is even more awesome than the statistics, though, is the program itself. After celebrating a memorial to Hiroshima Victims in Helsinki on August 6, the Peace Train, itself a public demonstration of international bonding and cultural openness, will make stopovers in eight cities — in St. Petersburg, Russia; Kiev, Ukraine; Bucharest, Romania; Sofia, Bulgaria; Istanbul, Turkey; Odessa, Ukraine; Alma-Ata, Kazakhstan; and Urumchi, China. In each of these places, Peace Train delegates will meet with women's groups. They'll discuss person-to-person, across continents and cultures, the issues of peace, justice and equality as they impinge primarily on the women of the area.

By concentrating on the women in each region, the Peace Train delegation makes a startling point about the silent linkage between women and violence everywhere: It is women and children who are the real victims of war, the silent casualties of militarism, the invisible scapegoats of budget cuts made to enhance the military budgets of the world, the bleeding quarry of the rapes now defined as legitimate weapons of the war machine. It is women and children who suffer most from the wars men fight to "defend" them while they talk about the patriotism and nationalism and "honor" that they prefer to fight out rather than to talk out.

The Peace Train points dramatically to the real reason that it is necessary to have an international conference on women in the first place. No one, after all, would think of having an international conference on men. The fact is, however, that when men have conferences, it is men who make decisions about male concerns. Seldom, if ever, does the discussion either include women – who are almost never treated as moral agents by either church or state – or refer directly to the effect of these male decisions on the lives of women and children. Women and their concerns are not "fit matter" for male decision-making, it seems, except perhaps in the most generic sense.

It is time to hear those voices and right that balance.

The Woman's International League for Peace and Freedom (WILPF), established during the period of the formation of the League of Nations and still headquartered in Geneva, is intent on drawing the consciousness of this reality to the attention of the world. For 80 years, the women and men of WILPF have been pressing nations to seek peaceful resolution to conflict. Marilyn Clement, WILPF'S Executive Director and US Section Coordinator, says "In 1995 we will be facilitating meetings of women whose countries are in conflict to offer support for non-violent solutions. On the Peace Train and in Beijing, WILPF will be calling on the governments of all the nations in the world to reduce their military budgets by at least 5% per year to provide at least 25% more resources for human development by the year 2000."

It is a paltry sum for which to beg for so long a time. Its very insignificance may indicate best the serious disregard of women's needs worldwide. It is interesting, for instance, that many of the men in our own Congress who increase military monies routinely, even as they tell unemployed mothers that we can no longer afford to give them welfare money, are the same men who tell women at the same time that women should be at home with their children. No wonder we need an International Conference on Women.

You will hear from me next from somewhere in the middle of a Russia deep in the throes of economic transition. The question to be considered there is, are women better off or worse off as a result of it? "There is nothing enduring in the life of a woman," Judith Anderson wrote, "except what she builds in a man's heart."

And Joseph Conrad said, "Being a woman is a terribly difficult task since it consists principally in dealing with men." Both ideas give a person pause. Is there nothing that women can do to change their own condition in the world? Are men closed to the needs of the other half of the world? As we go along, I'll let you know how it looks from here.

Helsinki

I am on the last leg of the flight into Helsinki now, the first step on the road to Beijing. I think of all the Bob Hope-Bing Crosby road shows and smile. I must remember to sing and dance a little, too, along the way. This is serious stuff we're doing, true, but not so serious that there shouldn't be a bit of play in it. That's the problem with revolutionaries, I have to remind myself. They can get too serious about things. They forget to recharge their energies and nourish their souls along the long, unending roads to social change. The problem is that you can't be in the business of global evolution for the sake of success; you can only come with hope. But to nourish hope, you need to play a little. Otherwise, what proof can we ourselves possibly give that life holds happiness at all?

The Women's International League for Peace and Freedom has launched a project in conjunction with the United Nations Fourth International Conference on Women that would give pause to the sturdiest of mountain climbers, the strongest of pioneer-types. This group has arranged to go from their international congress in Helsinki to the United Nations Conference in Beijing by train. They will cover over 6000 miles, take over 23 days to do it and visit women's groups in eight countries and nine cities along the way – Helsinki, St. Petersburg, Kiev, Bucharest, Sofia, Istanbul, Odessa, Alma-Ata and Urumchi. I will write as we go. Articles, yes, but also a personal journal, "An American Woman Meets the World" kind of thing. In the journal I'll record what I'm thinking and experiencing as a person in addition to what I finally say in the articles as professional observer and analyst. I can see it now: parochial in its perspective, pitiably simple, full of questions, rife with ignorance. Well, my limited self and my even more limited perspectives – formed in the West out of a Western bias and a Western insularism, but wild with a Western sense of risk, openness and undaunted wonder – are all I have to work with, so that will have to be enough. Surely Marco Polo had no more than that to gauge what he saw, what he felt, what it said to him and what, as far as he could tell, it might mean to the rest of the world around him.

I boarded the first plane in Erie, Pennsylvania with a sheaf of background materials and I haven't stopped reading yet. I am reading statistics about women from every corner of the globe. I am reading their statements and their cries for help. I am trying to think beyond my world to what it can possibly mean when they tell me that two-thirds of the illiterate of the world are women, that women die from malnutrition in percentages far beyond the men of their societies, that women are being bought and sold like cattle. It is depressing reading. How can it possibly be true? In a few instances, maybe, in extreme circumstances, perhaps, but not routinely, surely, are women misused, misvalued, degraded. After all, women are people.

But women all over the world report the same things: violence, dislocation, diminishment not simply because life is hard where they are but because they are women and it is hard to be a woman anywhere. Men thrive in every society. Women thrive in no society. Everywhere they are secondary, overlooked, domesticated like the animals around them. It is a litany of pain. I'm not even sure that I can bear being steeped in this material day after day for six weeks. After all, women themselves learn to ignore this material all their lives, to close their minds to the inequity called woman, to give it divine intent, if for no other reason than to stay sane. We talk about "God's will" for us and "a woman's role" and "woman's lot in life." We tell our intelligent daughters that intelligence is something they should pursue on the side, and we tell our athletic daughters that athletics is a pastime, not a life for them and we tell our assertive daughters that management is a man's task but that housekeeping is their task. We don't always tell them in so many words anymore, but they get the message, nevertheless. When there are no sports scholarships for women, they get the message. When there are no promotions for women, they get the message. When there are no high-salaried professorships for women, they get the message. When there are no full-time jobs for them with full-time benefits, let alone promotions and salary increases, they get the message. When his job and his diet and his interests supersede hers, again and again and again, they get the message. When they find themselves working two jobs – one to help pay the bills and the other to maintain the home – while he does only one, they get the message.

And is any of it really reversible? Why go to Beijing at all?
What has ever really changed for women? Women got the vote
and nothing changed. Women got jobs and nothing changed.
Women got education and nothing changed. All the structures simply adjusted to a new form of sexism. So what is the real problem?

August 6, 1995

Helsinki is a stiffly clean, ordered, modern city set in the middle
of forests and fjords. It's a European city – complete with pedes-
trian malls and street entertainers. And yet, somehow it's not European at all. It does not seem to bustle. It is not gloriously ancient.
It seems to be almost as much contemporary Russian as it is Finn-
ish. There is an assembly-line look to the rows and rows of apart-
ment buildings, a kind of one-size-suits-all universal city plan.
They eat outside in open-air plazas and talk English. They serve
Mexican food and charge horrendous prices for basic services.
They are citizens of the world.

I got here but my luggage did not. Why am I not surprised?
Lost luggage has got to be about par-for-the-course on a trip of
this scope. I did not expect everything to be perfectly placid for
so massive an undertaking and, unfortunately, I was not disappointed. They say they will send it to the hotel as soon as it
arrives. I have a distinct memory of a traveling companion of mine
being told that same thing on a similar kind of trip a few years
ago, and she got back to the States three weeks before her luggage did. I also have a memory of one of those great travel jokes
that people like me tell ourselves to remain calm in the middle of
chaos. "Once upon a time," the story goes, "a traveler rushed up
to the airline desk, breathless and shouting, 'I want this suitcase to
go to Dallas, this one to go to New York and this one to go to
Quebec.' 'I'm sorry, sir, but we are not permitted to separate a
passenger and his luggage like that,' the clerk said. 'Oh, really?'
the traveler said. 'Well, you did it to me yesterday on the way
out.' "

It's going to be a long trip. I have to keep laughing. Or at
least smiling when I can't laugh. Or at least not frowning when
I can't smile. Joan, once more now – with feeling – repeat after
me. . . .

The conference center is swarming with women from every continent, every country. There is a row of offices here, all designed to do impossible things efficiently, but whatever the good will that undergirds the place, good will is no substitute for information. And of that there is very little. Everyone gives everyone a different answer for everything. "Should we buy the new meal tickets?" Yes and no. "Should we pay in traveler's checks or cash?" Yes and no. "Are we still crossing the Baltic by boat?" Yes and no. "Are we finally going to get our Chinese visas as we were told we would?" Yes and no. Which means, as it has for weeks, "Yes, you will eventually get Chinese visas but – no, you will not get them here."

The important thing to do at a time like this is to refrain from asking questions at all. And if you must ask, for the sake of some kind of American compulsion for precision and accuracy, don't expect an answer. Good. Now that that's established, we can get on with the trip.

We walked through knots of women from one group to another for hours today, trying to get registered, directed, identified, and logged in, and I'm still not sure that I am on the right lists going to the right place, but no one else seems to know either so why should I worry?

Things are hysterically expensive in Finland. Or at least I got hysterical about them. They claim to give free social services but, believe me, you pay for them in lots of other ways, like tariffs and consumer taxes, for instance. It cost $2.50 for a one-way metro ticket to go about half-way to the meeting site and another $7.50 for a one-way ticket on the bus that followed it. And, after that, we walked for the last-half mile through a series of winding, empty streets and a thicket of ancient trees simply to pick up our train tickets at the WILPF convention site miles out of town and be welcomed together in one room. It was a flurry of costumes and cultures and languages. Welcome to the global turnstile. All aboard for the Tower of Babel. Welcome to Flagship Earth where nothing is what you may think you have reason to expect. Inside the door of the conference center, for instance, the first thing they handed me was a manila envelope full of condoms, a hundred of them, to distribute to health personnel in various places. "I am in the wrong crowd," I thought. "Someone here has me mixed up with somebody else." But, at the same time I had to admit that the stark reality of the situation brought all the material I'd been

reading about the issues facing Third World women into the kind
of sharp focus that no committee report had been able to do
nearly so effectively. I put the envelope in my shoulder bag for
three reasons: 1) the lady who had given the envelope of condoms to me was already far gone on her errand of mercy; 2) no
one else would take it, and 3) I couldn't bring myself to simply
leave it behind. (Good Catholic training, ironically.) Now all I have
to do is to try not to die in front of some bishop with condoms in
my backpack.

The orientation meeting of Peace Train participants was a series of welcomes in halting English and fluent French, all of them
without benefit of translation. But language didn't seem to matter
much. Women sat patiently on the steps as well as in the theater
seats of the overcrowded arena, applauded approvingly, listened
intently anyway. The audience in the auditorium ranged from very
old women – women too old for the rigors of this trip, I thought –
to very young ones – too young to be able to afford it. It was a
grand gathering of womanhood, all of whom have had enough of
violence, enough of repression, enough of docile patience, enough
of servile deference to the powers behind human destruction to
ever tolerate it again without protest.

"This train route has never been run before," one of the organizers announced, "in the history of world travel. . . ." I have
no doubt. Why would anyone go by train from Helsinki to Beijing, through eight countries with 230 women from 42 different
nations? Why, indeed, if not for life – to touch it and call for it
and demand it.

The theme of the meeting, the speakers remind us, is "Women
Crossing Borders" – political ones, personal ones, cultural ones –
none of them easy, none of them to be taken for granted. Some
women still waited for the Chinese to issue visas they had been
refusing to issue for months, while Chinese bureaucrats waited for
"instructions" from somebody somewhere to change the document
release date from August 5 to August 4. "Silly," the Americans said.
"Ridiculously incompetent," we huffed. But that is surely too simple an analysis by far. Incompetency is a personal and professional affliction, not a national disease. The explanation for the
bottleneck over hundreds of visas loomed far more sophisticated
than the singular nonpreparedness of a few underlings in local
Chinese consulates. No, the explanation for the visa problem is
certainly more complicated than that. The fact is that China is a

totalitarian state. Totalitarian Communism, you remember at a time like this, claims to be built on equality but actually settles all authority at the top.

The term "bureaucrat" in a democratic country is usually defined to mean a person who assumes too much authority over too little substance. A bureaucrat in a totalitarian nation, on the other hand, is someone who functions as a kind of robot of the system and has no authority at all. "We do not have instructions," became a byword for the whole visa process all the way up the line to the very highest of Chinese officials. No one had the necessary instructions from the Chinese Organizing Committee in Beijing to release the visas before the arbitrarily decided upon time of August 5 for a train that was leaving on August 4. No one on site had the authority to make a decision about the obvious. Whoever did have the authority was either hiding or yet to be born.

Whatever the cause, however, I began to think long and hard about the ease with which Americans move around the world and the pressure we put on other people who are trying to enter our own country as "undesirable aliens," that list of people we do not want. We require a letter of invitation to justify their coming through, we want to know about their bank accounts to make sure that they do not become wards of the state once they get into the country. Some industrialized nations even give tests that the people they don't want are unable to pass in order to control the number of non-whites they admit each year and look "fair" while they're doing it. While millions of refugees roam the world, welcome nowhere, the Chinese did us the favor of giving us a glimpse of powerlessness and undesirability. It was not a totally useless part of the trip.

We walked the dark cobblestone streets, ate in restaurants with "reindeer" on the menu – not easy for someone raised on " 'Twas the night before Christmas . . ." – and stopped at sidewalk cafes where blackjack dealers and street-corner entertainers were as common as coffee shops and newsstands in the US. In the fresh, Northern outdoor night, surrounded by lively students and quiet aging couples, it was easy to forget that miles away from these old cobblestone malls, women all over the world waited for us to speak a word on their behalf.

I have decided to "have a wonderful time" on this tour, whatever harsh conditions and confusing circumstances and frustrating

situations we find ourselves in. I can hardly wait to see how long
the resolution lasts.

August 7, 1995

The day train out of Helsinki is churning under us with that dogged
persistence that trains have: steady, somnolent, hypnotic. A few
voices in the car challenge the quiet of it, but not many. Most of
the car has succumbed to the rhythm of the train and sunk into a
kind of waking sleep. These women have been up since 4:00
a.m., preparing for an early departure. For many of them, this is
not the beginning of their journey. It is simply the piece of it
between their International Congress in Finland and the UN Conference in Beijing. They're tired and subdued far beyond the normal for an event of this magnitude. One woman, I am happy to
note, is already giving lectures to whomever will listen. The fact
that few people are even awake, let alone interested, deters her
not. Now here is the kind of zealot the world needs if change is
ever to come.

Everybody packed "light" – in my own case, a backpack, one
stewardess case and a two-pound computer – for a trip that will
last almost seven weeks. Even at this stage of the journey, however, few people can handle their bags alone. It takes three
women at a time to lift one another's suitcases and duffle bags
onto the overhead racks, straining and grunting all the way. The
papers and buttons and souvenirs are already beginning to pile up
and we have not even begun. This may be an interesting trip but
it is not going to be a simple one.

It's not difficult to tell who's from where, however. The North-
erners on the train are dressed in shorts and T-shirts, oblivious of
both the rain and the unseasonable drop in temperature; the
Southerners are huddled in jackets and slacks. For the Southerners,
the clothes they brought to stay cool in China are already too light
to keep them warm, and they are hoping for a desert or two
along the way. "There are very few facts out there," Gail, my
traveling companion, says. "Just a lot of different interpretations of
them." Obviously. But it is one thing to apply the concept where
the weather is concerned. It boggles the mind, however, when
you extend the notion to the realm of international politics. I
looked at the sweating/freezing travelers around me and winced a

little at the thought of how difficult it is going to be to discuss peace and women's issues in nine different cultures.

Hundreds of women who had attended the WILPF Conference but who were not going on to Beijing came to the train station to wave us off. They carried banners denouncing French nuclear testing and sang peace songs in languages I did not understand. I felt a little like the mouse that roared. Should we be crowing with the satisfaction that comes from speaking up against unspeakable odds? Or should we have the grace to blush with embarrassment at the very thought that 230 women could be players on the international stage of global politics, an arena long closed to women by both states and churches and long deprived because of that closure? Well, I thought as I looked out the window, the audacity of confronting the world with banners and songs – like Don Quixote in a fit of insane idealism, perhaps – may be embarrassing but it is moral imperative nevertheless. So off we go. Singing.

The cold and sore throat I never get at home has started here in the dampness of Helsinki. And the medicine chest is laughingly empty. I have pills for malaria, pills for diarrhea, pills to ward off allergies and pills to handle pain. But I brought absolutely nothing to cure the common cold. It's looking like it will be a normal trip. I have plenty of what I don't need; little of what I do.

"It's so nice that there's no Iron Curtain anymore," someone comments in the understatement of the year. "No," I think, "there's no Iron Curtain anymore. There's just a scrim of humanity across Eastern Europe, claiming a multitude of distinct national differences that underneath are all the same in the need for water, the desire for food, the struggle for resources, the illusory search for the Holy Grail of wealth." We are going to Beijing in behalf of women – but not only and not really. We are going to Beijing in behalf of life for that portion of the world least equipped to guarantee it for themselves – women and children caught in the economic breakdowns brought on by male power games everywhere.

St. Petersburg

St. Petersburg was an exercise in chaos. Women strained and groaned and carried luggage down what I thought was an endless railroad platform, sure that there would now be at least a few hours of quiet to walk the banks of the River Neva in the cool Russian evening before the first of the Peace Train programs began the next day. Wrong: We never even got to check in at the hotel before being whisked to the opening event of the visit. Buses with color-coded window markers – green, yellow, purple, white, blue – are already a regular part of our lives. We were herded by bus from the hotel to the train station in Helsinki and now swept off the train and put on the appointed buses again like young ducks following a blue mother hen into the middle of a great lake. Blue is the color. Never mind the destination; just follow the color. Blue bus, blue flag, blue identification tag, blue wagon on the train. Thank God for color coding instead of numbers. This one I can do.

But efficiency system or not, time was at a premium. In the course of the train trip from Helsinki to Petersburg, the Russian officers had checked our passports but then neglected to return them before our train pulled out. Every passport on the train had been left behind at the customs station on the Finnish-Russian border. Passports, we now knew after arm-wrestling with the Chinese about them for months, are the secret weapon of international diplomacy. We couldn't do a thing without them. Areas as close to one another as New Jersey to New York are closed to one another without the little piece of paper that declares citizenship, sovereignty, and control by one nation rather than another. There was nothing for our train to do, therefore, but to sit on a railroad siding between somewhere and nowhere for half an hour, waiting for the next train to catch up to us and deliver our passports back into our individual hands before we went on.

When we arrived in St. Petersburg, late, the Russian organizers were waiting for us. Plans were already changed. We were to attend the traditional Russian welcoming ceremony immediately. No change of clothes, no quick shower, no quiet night. Just slow speeches and slower translations of standard-brand introductory statements. One of them, unfortunately, the most standard brand of them all: The local male dignitary graced the group only long enough to welcome 230 of the most intelligent, best-educated and most experienced women in the world with the comment, "Having all you beautiful women here makes our city even more lovely." Then he sat down and flipped through a magazine on stage while women officials spoke of substantial things. The message was painfully clear: women are bodies to him and he was bored being part of something so unimportant. They call it sexism where I come from. And they clearly called it sexism in this auditorium. The audience groaned out loud. They had just been welcomed as "beautiful," – as females – rather than as intelligent or professional women – as humans. It was a tough moment – one of those tests of personality and perseverance that can strain relationships to the breaking point. But this crowd met the test. Old finishing school anthems came in handy: Smile and wave; smile and wave; smile. Whatever you do, smile. And we did. But the applause for the man was only lukewarm and nobody, absolutely nobody, laughed at the comment.

We walked up and down the old palace stairs at the meeting site as if for this crowd a trek from one side of the world to the other in three days was a bi-weekly event. I didn't count the number of steps. I didn't want to know how many there were for fear I would figure out thereby that I couldn't possibly manage them. And anyway, older women than I were doing it without a word of complaint. It is no time to plead fatigue when the woman next to you is climbing a hundred steps with a cane.

Everyone I tried to talk to around me, all of them also passengers on the Peace Train, answered in an English thick with accents from one end of the earth to the other. I, on the other hand, spoke hardly a word of their languages. This meeting was not going to be your average neighborhood get-together. I made a mental note to listen very carefully when people spoke to me on this trip and not to go drifting off into one of those philosophical reveries to which I am so commonly given. If I miss what's said here, nobody is going to repeat it for me, and if they do I must remember, whatever I do, not to trust the translation.

The hotel, when we finally got to it, was like everything else Russian – bigger than life and far too huge to negotiate with ease. Our side of the corridor alone had over 100 rooms on it, all of them small, all of them sparse. The beds in each room were hardly as wide as army cots. And nothing worked: not the toilet, not the telephone line, not the lamps, not the windows, not the doorknob. It was a first-class hotel, they told us. The thought boggled the mind. If this was first-class here, what was to be said about the class level that came with living in the United States?

There was newness in the air, however. This time, unlike my earlier experiences of Russia, I realized that there were no soldiers on every corner, no talk of fear, no barely disguised anti-Americanism. The Russians hardly noticed us. They didn't care where we went or what we did. There were no doorkeepers at every hotel entrance, no military in the lobby. We weren't in the house of the enemy this time. This time we were in the middle of a society confused about itself and more uncertain about its future than it was when it lived in the eye of a doomsday number of nuclear warheads. The women were especially forthcoming. It was a stark change.

On an earlier peace-making mission with the Fellowship of Reconciliation, the Russian women were quite emphatic with us about the fact that they were fully integrated into Soviet society: They worked, they were on all state commissions and committees, they earned exactly the same amount that men did. Russian women were completely equal to men. I doubted it then and I doubt it still. Nevertheless, I knew immediately that things had certainly changed for women here in the intervening years. And, hard as it was for the West to imagine – or admit – the change had been for the worse. Freedom had not freed women.

At long sessions the next day, it was one story after another of women made purposely poor. The new economic system had put industry into the hands of private owners, the women told us, who then trimmed the workforce to increase profits rather than to spread the wealth. The workers who have been let go in Russia are almost universally women. It is a shocking example of male power supporting male systems and keeping systems male. All at one time, all in one place the operational theory of the rest of the universe has been made very plain. Clearly, men have decided that despite the educational level of these most educated of women, despite their years of professional experience under the

Soviet system, despite their established competency, women are to be in the home, women are to be economically dependent on men, women are to be wards of the society, not contributors to it. How very convenient for men.

There were tables set up in the foyer outside the meeting rooms in which we were gathered. While we all sat inside, talking about the economic situation of women in the new democratic, capitalistic Russia, women stood outside the large, old double doors of the room, next to the tables waiting for us to come out. The tables, some of them sparse, some of them over-crowded, held local arts and crafts – painted bread boards, crocheted scarves, trinkets – the work of simple women from the country-side, I thought as I went in to the session. But inside the meeting room, the panelists told us otherwise: One table carried the work of a woman whose doctorate was in engineering, another one held items done by a past government economist. A third table carried a little lace done by an accountant. Other women, all un-employed, all professionals, milled around the area, prodding us to look, to handle, to buy. I picked up a hand-painted bread board. Good wood. Fine art. Hours of work. Two dollars each. I felt a kind of shame worm its way through me. This was not right. This was not women doing business. These were women looking for a handout: like musicians in a subway playing Bach. I was too embarrassed to look at them. I put the breadboard back on the table and, when no one was looking, slipped ten dollars under it and moved quickly away.

With no time left before the train pulled out again, we took one of those see-nothing bus trips through the streets of St. Peters-burg while one of the recycled Intourist Guides, once the official purveyors of the Party Line, now proud patriot of the new Russia, pointed out the Hermitage Museum and great old cathedrals, now museum attractions, and once-state-controlled "museums" which had now become working cathedrals again. Children crowded around the buses to sell traditional Russian nesting dolls, and I bought a set. What do I need with nesting dolls? Not a thing.

The River Neva that flowed past the czars and past the cos-saks and past the commissars flowed just as unperturbably through capitalist Russia today. But it was a different Russia, I realized. In this Russia, a professor in the Women's Studies Department at a local university had pointed out to us in the morning session, there is not even a word for "domestic violence," and the woman who attempts to prosecute a man for battery or even to divorce him may find herself, for reasons of the Russian housing shortage, forced to go on living not only in the same flat with him but in the same room as well. I remember the gasp that went through the room as the translator droned the passion out of that information. I sat there and remembered pregnant relatives who could not leave abusive men because there was no way for a woman to support a family in those days. I hear it all around me still on the inner-city street on which I live. But not even to have a word for it in the language is to indicate that it is not a concept in the culture. To beat a women is not a type of "violence" here. "Domestic violence" is not any violence at all. It simply is. I sat there and wondered if the Russians have a phrase for "cruelty to animals." But then, I wasn't sure that I really wanted to know.

We stopped to take pictures at a restored Byzantine church and I ran out of film just before I was about to take what I was sure would be the best picture in the city. I can see that my luck hasn't changed yet. It is still god-awful. I moved across the street to a small open-air market and bought a hand-carved chess set from the young man who had carved it. This could, after all, be a long, long trip. And not enough play makes Joan a dull girl.

All the tiny little Russian gingerbread houses between St. Petersburg and Kiev rush by the train windows now, small and poor and old. The newly dissolved Soviet Union is no longer a country focused on war. No, things are worse than that now. The newly independent countries of the region must in this period begin to think about the challenges of living when there is no enemy except themselves to face.

The nice thing about outside enemies, any good history teacher knows, is that they keep a country from focusing on internal problems. If a government is lucky – and smart – mobilization can even make deprivation seem like a privilege to people. It takes no small amount of talent, however, to keep people devoted to "the war effort" in peacetime. In Russia, apparently, they failed. In the United States they did not. In the United States, we are still capable of spending more money on instruments of destruction than we do on human development. Even in the States, though, it can't last forever. Either Americans will eventually see through it, recognize the stranglehold it has on medical care, on education, on social development, and demand a social change, or our own system, like this one we were looking at now, will finally fall under its own weight. What else is all this talk about national debt and deficit anyway except that we have spent ourselves into a military hole that we are now blaming on food stamps? We won the arms race and lost that quality of society that made us unique in all the world. Now the Japanese, whom ironically we would not permit to militarize, have the infrastructure and social services that we lack. The Irish say, "We laugh because we cannot cry." Well, we better learn to laugh. And soon.

I got about three hours sleep last night. Supper at the Moskva Hotel was late, long and complete with floorshow, one of those great Russian extravaganzas that is part circus, part American rock. It ended with the crowd doing a congo line through the tables that started with "When the Saints Go Marching In" and ended with "Chattanooga Choo Choo." Gail, my Irish companion, had doffed her heavy red sweater and was at the head of a vigorously moving line. I got the idea that she had done a lot of these lines before.

Sitting at a table over in the far corner of the room, wearing a Penn State sweatshirt, was the man who later came out in a tux and black tie to MC the show. A graduate of Penn State, the Nittany Lion was the last thing I expected to see in St. Petersburg. I looked at the sweatshirt and wondered how either the shirt or I had gotten from the "Corner Room" in State College, Pennsylvania to this ballroom on the Baltic Sea. Have no doubt about it: the world we were born in is not the world we live in.

I spent three hours after the show squeezed between my bed and an old water heater trying to send an e-mail message down the Russian phone lines. The plan was to figure out the European system here before I found myself somewhere else in Eastern Europe trying to meet a last-minute deadline, only to find out that I didn't know how to make a connection. After all, I figured that if I could connect anyplace in Eastern Europe, Russia would be the best place to do it, and that what I learned here would enable me to get on-line everywhere else along the rest of the route. The spectacle had all the earmarks of a scene out of a World War II spy movie where the hero tries desperately to make a ham radio work in the middle of the German High Command. The only difference was that I never did make the connection. Not to the wall, not to the wires, not to the phone. Nothing worked: not the adapter, not the coupler, not the alligator clips. This was, at best, a nice basic 1970 phone system. And this is the country, I was told, that was so technologically sophisticated, so dangerous that the United States lived in constant peril from them. This was the country we used to justify our own giant war machine and its assault on everything decent in society, every dimension of social life, every human need. I put the tools away hours later and wondered if the paper would ever hear another word from me, either from this part of the world or the next.

After another morning of conversation with Russian women and workshops on the effects of *perestroika* on women, their employment problems and the need for re-education, we did those things that tourists do – only faster. We jumped off buses to take pictures of places we never really saw, bargained with young capitalists selling on the streets now what used to be available only in the *beriozskas* – the outlet stores for tourists that the Soviet government used to bring Western currency into a country that did not trade in the money markets of the world – and dragged hundreds of pounds of luggage down yet one more railroad line. The station was dirty, crowded, full of smoke and a swirling eddy of people going every direction at once. But soot or no soot, I never saw anything in my life that looked better than this train.

The Peace Train is our very own chartered 16-car house-on-wheels for the next 21 days. It is clean but not sparkling, quiet but not soundproofed and maliciously, invidiously, outrageously small. A cabin for two is about 6 feet wide by 7 feet long. A cabin for four is the same. And it's wonderful. All this quiet to ourselves. All this privacy to ourselves. All this time to ourselves. Whoever said that hermitages are a deprivation of the human spirit? After days of walking and days of packing and days of going from one place to another every night, this place is a little piece of heaven, a tiny slice of home. At least now. How long women stacked in fours, like shoe boxes on the wall of a small closet – the configuration of most of the cars on this train – can last, I don't know. All I know is that I hope that being in a two-person compartment will enable me to last at least long enough to get there with – how do the lawyers put it? – "sound mind and able body." Selfish, I know, but honest anyway.

St. Petersburg

The Peace Train with its 230 delegates to the Fourth UN Conference on Women in Beijing is grumbling along toward the Ukrainian border now, past patch after patch of villages grown up like wild flowers along the route. All of them are somberly the same: There are no streets in them, only mud paths between the houses; no water lines, only pumps and wells; no landscaping, no sewage, no cars.

The country which the United States was led to believe was the technological wonderland of the 20th century in order to justify our own military economy stands poor and underdeveloped in front of us. There are foresters with hand tools, and old women tending goats, and row after row of gingerbread houses with corrugated roofs. It seems to be a strange place to even think of having discussions about things so erudite as UN draft documents on women and global liberation movements. But it is not. This is exactly what the women's movement is really all about. And all the women on this train, stereotypical images, some would say, of what we like to think of as a white Western fad — posh, manicured, middle-aged, cultivated and rebellious — know it.

The truth is that if the image of feminists in either church or state is that feminism is superficial, something that will disappear with the next generation, the next new intellectual fling, the image is wrong. Feminism, it seems, is something that does not go easily away, is disturbingly perduring, is everywhere now and cuts across all cultures and all age levels. There is an 80-year-old woman on this train. There is a woman on crutches who has walked every set of steps to every meeting. There are young women from everywhere — from Sweden and Germany and India and Africa and Baltimore. There are women from 42 separate countries from Oceania to Vancouver, Canada on this train. For the first time in history, feminism has begun to find its global self. Yesterday, in St. Petersburg, we saw a face of it that touched far too many nerves.

In 1989, on a previous delegation, the Russian women we met with then told us with vehemence that they had no problems: Communism had made them equal, they said. They were just like the men, they said. They didn't even know what we were talking about when we asked them what life was like for women in the Soviet Union. "Why, just like it is for men," they said.

If that was ever true, it certainly is not true anymore.

This time we heard the wails of women who have been displaced, made poor, ignored, rede-

placed, made poor, ignored, redefined as useless. With the advent of the market economy, industries reorganized — and women lost their jobs. Suddenly, in a society that had long known suffering, life took on a peculiarly precarious tilt for women. Questions that women in a Communist state never dreamed they would have to deal with arose with the ubiquity of surround-sound.

Education became a major problem: Should women go on being prepared for professions — science, business, professional work — they would possibly never attain again? Or, on the other hand, did women have any hope whatsoever in this new capitalist society if they were not highly educated? How could they even think of going on having children they could not support? How, in fact, could they support themselves? Women, they told us plaintively, are 70% of the unemployed in St. Petersburg alone. Some of them, past engineers and doctors, were now selling handicrafts in the lobby outside the very conference room in which we were discussing their situation.

After years of state-supported child care, state-paid family vacations, state-supplied housing, state-defined employment, state price controls and matching state pensions, the Russian woman has come face to face with discrimination and it has descended with a vengeance. Capitalism, Marx had taught, requires an underclass to make wealth for the higher class. Equality, it follows, is constitutionally impossible in a society where patriarchy, male control of all the major elements of society, and capitalism are mutually reinforcing concepts. In the capitalist society, someone is on top of a steadily enlarging bottom, and women are the bottom of the bottom. In a capitalist patriarchy, someone profits from being on top, and the people on top are male. Whatever the truth of the philosophical analysis, women in Russia have learned to their peril that "freedom" is at best a no-win game for women who have little or nothing from which to choose.

"Women over the age of 50," a professor of Women's Studies at St. Petersburg University told us, "live a social death. They have no property, no money, no children, no social contacts." Women have no reason to live. But they do. And society does very little about it. The same men who talk about cutting the social welfare payments of single mothers are also the same men who say that women should stay home with their children in our society as well as theirs.

The irony cuts to the bone. Russia is simply one more example of one more male revolution that did not help women. The men of the Western world told women that as soon as World War I was over, they would attend to the question of women's suffrage but women had to go to jail to get it. "As soon as we win our independence," Irish men told Irish women, "we'll concentrate on women's rights" – and the Irish Constitution still says that women belong in the home. As soon as we get desegregation, we'll concentrate on the rights of women, they said in the US Civil Rights Movement. And US women are still struggling for their civil rights. But this time, clearly, not alone. Women from all over the world are on their way to Beijing now, one unending stream of the invisible of the world demanding to be seen, to be heard, to be more than a bundle of "unique and special characteristics," to be fully human, human beings with all the right to make all the same mistakes that men have made all their lives. "The true Republic:" Susan B. Anthony printed on the front of her newspaper, *Revolution,* "Men, their rights and nothing more; women, their rights and nothing less."

The situation is getting clearer by the mile. Let both church and state beware. The revolution is among us still and it is not yet complete.

Kiev

The night on the train from Petersburg to Kiev was pure heaven. No telephone calls. No daily schedule to check. No preparations for the next day. Gail and I played a chess game and had a nice hour of simple Russian food in good company in a dining car all set with plastic flowers and linen tablecloths. Gail is a lawyer and family therapist who is trying to apply the principles of feminist theory to marriage counseling. Ruth is a clinical psychologist who works in multicultural programs at Colgate University. Mim is a 77-year-old Quaker-become-Methodist who has worked in the peace movement all her life. The saints are all around us. It is simply a matter of letting them into your life. The train abounds with women of this caliber. Most of all, it is the older women who are having the deepest effect on me. When I look at them, I realize that we are never permitted to give up. "You are not obliged to complete your work," the Talmud says, "but you are not at liberty to quit it." I'm lucky to be with such people.

We settled into the little cabin, counted our losses – Gail had left her sweater in the banquet hall in St. Petersburg, I had burned out a transformer – read awhile and went to sleep. The bunk is vinyl-covered wood, hard and narrow, and the cabin is minuscule but the night was cool and the train rocked us into blessed oblivion.

By the time I'd finished my dry porridge and written an article the next morning, we were in Kiev. It didn't take a genius to recognize the difference in the two places. Petersburg was beautiful and efficient and dour, a people stripped of power and prestige. Kiev was sunny and warm and alive, a country drunk with its new identity and promise. A military band, of all things, met this peace delegation at the railroad station playing national marches. I have never seen a better use of military money.

Ukrainian women in national costumes sang songs while they distributed the pieces of homemade welcome bread dipped in salt which, in this part of the world, wishes the guest all the necessi-

22

ties of life and all its spice, as well. It was a kind of global Eucharist, I thought, and as I took hold of a great warm nugget of it, I found myself thinking "Body of Christ." "Body of Christ" to Mickey, the Jewish woman who has given her life to the peace movement. "Body of Christ" to Manel, the Sri Lankan whose neighborhood was destroyed yesterday by Tamil suicide bombers. "Body of Christ" to all of these good women who were interrupting their own lives to speak for all the women of the world. It made me wonder whether it was this Eucharist that made the eucharistic liturgy authentic or the eucharistic liturgy that made this Eucharist possible. Maybe the real truth is that neither is true without the other.

The Hotel Bratislava, our guidesheet pointed out euphemistically, "would not reflect American standards." That's one way to put it. But the sheets were clean and the water was hot. My sense of "standards" gets lower every day. And it gets higher at the same time. What gets even clearer than that, however, is the fact that most of the world lives at this other level. And under it all runs the question that plagues the world: Are we in the West unjust in our control of resources and therefore rich at their expense or are they simply less enterprising than we are and so poorer than they should be? In the Ukrainians I got a hint of the answer, I think. I find a standard of simplicity and industry here that no amount of slick technology can match for quality of life.

Kiev is one of a series of Ukrainian cities starved out by Stalin in 1932, bombed to smithereens during World War II and now struggling to recover independence in the wake of the dissolution of the Soviet Union. What's more, they are trying to survive Chernobyl, the Russian disaster on Ukrainian territory. Ukrainians survived the Holocaust despite Stalin's attempts to obliterate them. They recovered from the bombing of World War II in record time and rebuilt the entire center of the city with massive and monumental architecture. There is not a doubt in my mind, if what we saw here is in any way typical, that they will also survive the legacy of death now recently inherited from the explosion in the Russian nuclear reactor at Chernobyl as well.

There was something in our Ukrainian experience that was different and it took me a while to identify it. In the first place, we were women, but we were important enough to be met by a state band, conducted by police escort – always a show of dignity in this part of the world – and hosted in government dining rooms. This morning we were addressed by almost every Minister of Government in the chambers of the Ukrainian Parliament itself, in a building full of crystal chandeliers, Persian rugs and marble staircases, as if what we thought and what we did really mattered. I tried to imagine a group of women being met in Washington, D.C., with such respect.

Clearly, it's not what people say that counts most in the description of a person's real status. It's what they do because of what they say they think that matters. The Ukrainians, by treating us as fully functioning adults, partners in the process of being human, afforded us humanity without saying a word about it. The church, at least mine, on the other hand, says all manner of exalted things about women, but it never really exalts women to the level of humanity that men take for granted. It doesn't listen to us; it doesn't recognize our relationship to God; it doesn't entrust to us the theological definitions of our soul. It does not make us part of any deliberating body that purports to weigh the spiritual insights of the human race. When, over the first meal of choice we had had in days, I shared the thought with Gail, she cocked her head, arched her eyebrows, pulled down the corners of her mouth and said whimsically "Hmmmm, very good, Joan. This soup's gone right to your head, I see." I got the message: To even imagine that such a thing should happen would be considered daft. Maybe, but true nevertheless.

The workshops in Kiev were sad testimony to a nation sacrificed to another people's greatness. The whole situation smacked of the days of Imperial Rome and the conquered territories, of England and Spain and the colonial blight on modern history. Ukraine, once the nuclear dumping ground of the Soviet Union, found itself left to clean up what it had not created. In a particularly poignant move, the meeting opened with a moment's silence to commemorate the victims of Hiroshima and Nagasaki. I felt the way a German must feel who is asked to remember the victims of the Holocaust. It was a Christian nation, my own, that invented the end of the world and stores it in the cornfields of Kansas. It was a Christian nation, my own, that had unleashed the technology that was now, little by little, destroying this nation, too.

They are surrounded by death. Missile sites defile the land; the failed nuclear reactor at Chernobyl poisons the people. Thyroid cancers have increased 100% since the nuclear power plant disaster, birth defects are common now, valuable farm land deteriorated under radioactive pollution. "We are a dying society now," the Minister for the Environment reported. "Be envoys for us. We need help."

Veiled by that statement lay the failure of the United States to honor the 1991 Nunn-Lugar treaty which promised $800,000,000 to help subsidize the dismantling of weapon sites in the Soviet Union, a situation very much in our own interests if we are really serious about arms control and nuclear disarmament. It was one more of those times when I cringed to be an American. By the end of 1994, we had released less than 14% of the money, most of it to Russia, and that for metal blankets to protect nuclear weapons in transit, none of it for dismantling anything, let alone decontaminating the area.

The thought haunts me: Have we made profit rather than good our national anthem? And is it affecting our own people now as much as it affects our foreign policy? What do Newt Gingrich and his company of wealthy brigands care about the health of anyone but their industrial supporters? What did the pirates care about the lives of the people who awaited the ships they stopped and plundered? What does the United States care about the condition of Ukrainian land and the children it feeds? Gingrich takes from the poor to satisfy the rich; our government breaks its treaties to honor its thirst for absolute power. It is a universal example of the dictum that those who take, get. We have seen the effects of governmental insensitivity before. Once it was called "The French Revolution." This time it is a global anti-Americanism that has erupted in the face of national devastation here and everywhere. The question is, of course, are we responsible for their problems? Are we their biblical keepers? Did we or did we not invent and unleash this evil on all the innocent of the world?

There were statistics to confirm the dying, of course. Forest lands had become a battleground in the great struggle between industrial interests trying to create a new economic base and environmentalists trying to save an already ravaged land. Unemployment was high, especially among women here, too, as it was in Russia. Waterways choked with industrial pollution and the populations with them. And the nation had no money to do anything about anything.

The list went on and on. But the list of social issues, as tragic as they are, was not what I took with me out of Ukraine. As the train pulled out of the station, the platform was lined with strong,

beautiful Ukrainian women, impressive figures all. I remembered
the beauty of the banquet they hosted for us the night before, the
smorgasbord of fresh-cooked Ukrainian specialties, the strength in
their words as they spoke, the incredible number of women's organizations they represented, the growing number of women in
government, the smart cut of their clothes, the firm ring in their
voices, the confidence in their dark eyes. Ukrainian women had
inherited three major disasters in the last 50 years and had recovered from them all. If anyone is going to preserve this country
again and enhance the status of women everywhere as they do it,
it will surely be women like these. On the other hand, it may be
precisely women like these who, like thousands of generations of
women before them, will be suppressed one more time as the
world races toward its extermination from the institutionalization
of solely masculine values.

I shuddered at the thought. I even felt one of those
wonderful surges of life-giving anger. The first thing a woman is
taught is that anger is not "nice," and that is precisely what en-
slaves her. Men, on the other hand, are taught that anger is
"manly," and that is precisely what puts them in control. Women
must come to realize that anger is what fuels us to change and
gives us the energy to persist. Anger is not bad. Anger can be a
very positive thing, the thing that moves us beyond the accep-
tance of evil. To be a feminist and not to be an "angry" feminist is
a shame, maybe even shameful. Holy anger is a moral imperative.
"If we had been holier people," Templeton says, "we would have
been angrier oftener."

The fact is that the loss of the feminine in life is not right, is
suicidal and must not be allowed to persist. No one should ever
come to peace with the rape of the minds and bodies and souls
of half the human race for the convenience of the minds and
souls and bodies of the other half. No matter how long it takes,
we must not give up the struggle for women's rights. The journey
to Beijing must be a new beginning, not an end.

"Honey, I'm ho-ome," Gail called laughingly down the corridor
to our wagon-mates as we boarded the train again. And home it
had become. It was time to be rocked in the cradle of the world
again, time for another game of chess, time for the sparse meals
and warm beer. Time to think about it all. Question: Will this trip
change women's lives? Answer: Only if it changes my own.

Bucharest

August 12, 1995

The train trip from Kiev to Bucharest tasted of old East European politics. We left Bulgaria with a passport check, entered Moldavia and had a passport check, moved again into Ukraine for another passport check and then prepared to cross the border into Romania. But going from Ukraine into Romania took a great deal more than a passport check. At about 4:45 a.m., soldiers opened every cabin door, did the perennial passport collection and left us with customs forms to fill out. I remember rubbing my eyes a second time and worrying about whether or not my eyesight was failing me before I realized that I couldn't read the forms because they were written in Romanian. And at 4:00 a.m., in the morning no less. Then, with the customs officers and the money-changers off the train, the greasers began the long, hard, slow process of dismantling the entire 16-car train, raising every wagon 15 feet into the air, and changing every set of wheels to satisfy the minuscule difference in railroad gauges designed to assert the uniqueness of Romania from all the other countries in Eastern Europe. I heard the clanging, squinted at the rising sun, handed over my passport one more time, copied down what everyone else had on the customs form, trusting that someone, somewhere on the train knew what the thing was saying and went straight back to sleep until 9:00 a.m. Others walked the platform, did exercises together and took Polaroid shots of young soldiers and older conductors, but not I. I don't know if it was heat, fatigue or just plain overload but I slept almost all day long until we arrived in Romania at about 7:00 p.m. My new motto: If you can't get away from a crowd, go to sleep in the middle of it.

The routine is getting to be second-nature: We were three hours late arriving in Bucharest. So, if you are late arriving you don't get to go to the hotel. Instead, hot and tired and sweaty, you are bustled off to the first meeting heavy with backpacks and money belts and cameras and, in my case, the computer. Then everybody does all the proper things, goes through all the protocols, talks in diplomatese and says nothing. Except for the fact that it gives a general first impression of a place, it has no value whatsoever. In this case, however, the first impression was the message.

"Dirty, dirtier, dirtiest" seems to be the plan for this trip. Every place we've been has been worse than the one before it. But it is not dirt that is the message; it is poverty. The two are invariably related. When people are poor, they buy bread, not soap; tortillas, not toilet paper; food, not furniture. And Bucharest is tragically poor.

The meeting center was one of those dirty, gray, box-like buildings with cavernous halls, gritty floors, smelly bathrooms, grimy windows and cheap, creaking furniture that had hardly a moment of glory, hardly any glory to celebrate for more than a moment. The Romanian women were lovely but poorly prepared for any kind of real meeting. The "translator" put strings of words together that had little or no relationship to one another and covered her embarrassment by looking askance at the speakers. Languages were no more a strength in this group than they are in the United States, and there were certainly no resources among these women for hiring professionals to provide translators. What's worse, whatever was being said in English, it could not be heard in the back of the crowded room. The loudspeaker system was a small one, and even adjusted to the hilt was hardly adequate for half the hall. The information was spotty and vague as a result, and the substance of it was lost on me almost entirely. I realized, though, that the women were speaking with passion about the effects of capitalism and war, the diminishment of women and the plight of refugees. I groaned inwardly. I had the feeling that we had come a long way to hear absolutely nothing about what we wanted to hear most, and to be hot and dirty while we did it. But I was dead wrong. There was a great deal more to be seen here, a great deal more to be learned that no amount of technical problems could hinder.

After the experience of the train station and the condition of the meeting site, the Doboranti Hotel in Bucharest was a complete conundrum. By Eastern European standards, it sparkled. There was hot water in the rooms, the beds were clean, the furniture was usable, the phones were American and the bathroom was spotless. I sent my e-mail with the kind of ease I take for granted in the United States and went to the dining room for a good supper –

meaning more than the dried-out cucumber, curled-up cheese and hard bread that were now the daily fare on the train. But the contrast between the hotel, and the hoved-up, pot-holed streets of the city and the poorly lit, broken-down conference hall begged for resolution. How were these extremes possible? The explanation wasn't long in coming.

I had chosen the workshop on "Women and Violence" for this week's concentration. I had focused on the train trip itself in my first article, then on the transition to a market economy in the second one about Petersburg and Kiev. I thought it was time to shift my attention to personal issues. It was in Bucharest that I came best to understand that one is the other.

Hardly 150 miles away from the war in Yugoslavia, Romanians are deeply affected by it. Goods and produce, imports and exports, once shipped either up or down the river, had now fallen victim to the boycotts and blockades of Yugoslavia. Tourism in the area had been deeply affected. People were not only avoiding the obvious war zones, they were staying clear of the entire region. Families were divided psychologically and emotionally by the situation. Some families had even lost relatives in the war itself. Refugees were straining the capacity of surrounding areas to absorb them. And violence against women was escalating in direct proportion to the frustration and economic instability in the society at large. "Our women have nothing," they said. "Nowhere to go; no one to help them. Here, if a woman leaves her family, she is disgraced. So she stays and is beaten again, over and over. We want to start shelters but we have no money. Tell us how to do it. Tell us what you did to begin."

What had been political issues in other places were deeply personal here. Romania was, for all intents and purposes, a prisoner of war held economically hostage to someone else's conflict. Its women most of all. But the war was not all the fault of a foreign invader.

There was even more of a lesson to come. The Doboranti Hotel demonstrated it with appalling accuracy.

This morning the meetings were held in the Romanian House of Parliament, The place affected me like few other things in my whole life. Sister Laura, my second-grade teacher, taught us that if we ever found ourselves in a dirty movie we should get up and leave it. This, I think, was a dirty movie that nobody has been able to leave.

The Romanian Parliament Building and the blocks of high-level condominiums leading to it is Nicolae and Helena Ceausescu's monument to megalomania. Believe me, Marco Polo should have died hereafter. I have never seen the likes of it and I doubt that he did either, all apologies to Kubla Khan, whose summer palace Polo described for the West. According to the Guinness Book of Records, Ceausescu's parliament is the largest building in Europe, second in the world only to the US Pentagon and larger than Cape Canaveral or the pyramids of Egypt. Worst of all, it is located in one of the poorest countries in Europe, with a population of 23 million and an average per capita annual income in US currency of $1650.

Designed in 1984 by a 26-year-old woman architect, it was three-quarters completed when the Ceausescu's were executed in 1989. The building itself came close to being destroyed in the revolution, so intense is the anger of the Romanian people in its regard. It had taken 20,000 workers working 16-hour shifts day and night to build it, and it cost 80% of the national budget to build. It is a monument to death: the death of the people, the death of the country, the death of the Ceausescu administration itself.

Every ceiling has a different style cut-glass chandelier. The largest hand-woven rugs in the world are in this building. There are 2500 light bulbs in one single room. Glass and hand-carved wooden "pocket doors," at least 20 feet high and 12 feet wide, separate the major wings. The amount of electricity needed to run the palace for one day equals the amount of electricity it takes to run the entire rest of the city. I was breathless in the place, full of awe, full of horror. The whole escapade made Ferdinand Marcos' political exploits look like the amateurish maneuvering of an international altar boy.

We sat and talked about violence against women – personal, domestic and structural – in a place that was itself a human obscenity. In 1995. Out on the streets of Romania, dirty was a way of life. Inside, here, posh was lower-class. I can hear the women yet. They know the problems. They are even gathering the statistics. They are unmasking the demon, to themselves and to the women around them. But they don't have a clue what to do about it. "We have never been allowed to organize," they said. "We don't know what to do."

At the railroad station, dirty beggar children crowded against us in grimy clothes with running sores on their unwashed heads. There was no money left for housing here. There was no money left to feed children here. There was no money left for education here. It had been spent on a monument to male ego. I felt my body crawl with the moral filth of it.

We're back on the train now, escaping Romania and its intrusion on our souls, left with our moralisms while we leave them with their problems. Tonight in Bucharest, the rich will go on eating fine meals in glitzy hotels and playing cards in casinos lit by the best chandeliers in Europe. The poor will eat little or nothing at all. In a country where women had been legislated as the "producers" of the society and made to bear at least five children for the nation and its workforce, women are now the poorest of the poor, the least protected, the most vulnerable to the changes taking place in society and the outbursts of the men who maintain the male system. Women will bear the burden of the violence that inhumanity breeds among humans. And the world will go on. The only question is, why? For our growth or to our peril?

Bucharest

Life for women in Eastern Europe is markedly different, distressingly the same as we have found for women everywhere.

When the Peace Train pulled out of Kiev, away from the ongoing aftermath of Chernobyl and its continuing Soviet legacy of death, I thought we had seen it all. I couldn't have been more wrong.

In Ukraine, people are struggling to save what had become the Russian dumping ground for nuclear waste and industrial pollution. The trees are gone, the waters are thick with industrial pollutants, whole portions of land are radiated, every woman faces the threat of bearing a child who will bear the scars of the world's second nuclear disaster. The conference on women opened, in fact, with a memorial moment for Hiroshima. I felt a kind of poignancy about the situation. In the United States, the indiscriminate bombing of civilians to save soldiers – the act that changed the nature both of war and of peace – is still a matter of pride. Hiroshima hardly touches the culture. Here, people know the effects of nuclearism as clearly as the Japanese do. "We are dying," the Minister of the Environment said. "We need help." And they do. And they're not getting it. Not even from countries like the United States who, in their own best interests, promised to subsidize the dismantling of nuclear re-

actors in treaty after treaty designed to end the arms race.

And yet, even with all of that, Kiev is a bright city. Its government is dotted with strong women. The women are not easily intimidated and few men, at least, claim to be listening to them. "Soon there will be more women than men in government," one of the male ministers said. "Men are selfish and seek power; women are noble and seek to save the world. It is the women we need now." The conclusion may well be a fair one. After all, these people have seen first hand the effects of machoism gone wild.

Without doubt, Kiev is a fractured place but not really a sad one, definitely not a hopeless one. Here, the sense of independence and pride and competence burned like a coal in winter.

In Bucharest, on the other hand, the voices of the women we met were just as strong but clearly more plaintive, definitely less sure. Romanians have been invaded by more than toxic waste.

In the city of Nicolae and Helena Ceausescu, rape is a way of life, first political and now personal as well. The political violations have been confronted and overcome – the Ceausescu's are gone – but the need to respond to the personal ones are only now beginning to dawn.

The Romanians are a people raped in the name of the nation by the father of the land. Nicolae Ceausescu, president of the country from 1965 to the time of the revolution in 1989, used the nation to enhance a megalomania of massive proportions. The House of Parliament in which we met demonstrated the national situation with painful clarity. The building is the largest in Europe, second in size in the entire world only to the Pentagon. Twenty thousand workers labored 16 hour shifts for slave wages to finish a monument that cost 80% of the country's national budget to build. The remaining 20% of the GNP went to all social programs of the whole country. Or, think of it this way: This building, which has 2500 light bulbs in one room alone, takes the same amount of electricity in one day that is allotted to all the rest of Bucharest put together. This mausoleum to ego-run-amok rises out of a city limited in resources, left without the basics of life and cast asea in economic drift. The revolution is over, the Ceausescu's are a thing of history, and the people are left with the squalor of the poor and casinos of the rich, both of which are still functioning at about the same level as they did before. What's worse, the war in Yugoslavia has choked off the bulk of Romanian trade as well.

In that social environment, women who claim the second highest level of education in Europe are finding themselves more and more displaced, more and more the victims of domestic violence, less and less able to deal with the problems. "We have never had private organizations before. We don't know how to do these things. We want to know how to start shelters, for instance. The police don't respond, the punishments aren't sufficient, the attitudes of men have to change," they said.

The social dimensions of the problem are pervasive here, too. Domestic violence crosses all levels of society, violence against women is on the increase, punishment is rare and shelters are overcrowded. Violence against women is a systemic war waged against the powerless with the implicit approval of the powerful. Wife-beating is on the increase in a region that is Christian, 86% Russian Orthodox.

Indeed the attitudes of men must be changed. But how will that ever be done in a world where religion continues to preach the superiority of men, the headship of male authority and God's rejection of women in sacred places?

The fact is that until the churches begin to teach otherwise, the church itself must bear a great deal of responsibility for the ongoing oppression of women. In the Roman church, we have a letter from the Pope now apologizing to women ". . . if objective blame, especially in particular historical contexts, has belonged to not just a few members of the church . . .," proclaiming the equality of women, and even praising the Women's Movement for its perspicacity in noticing this before anyone else did, apparently. It is a welcome addition to the literature of the church on women, of course, late as it is in coming. On the other hand, that same letter continues to define women as some kind of different species whose role is essentially biological rather than essentially human and who have no place in sacred space. The words of praise raise hopes but the underlying implications are deadly. The letter leaves women without full moral agency, in a place where men decide that men may decide who may live and who may die, what truth is and what the scriptures mean.

It is a nice letter, but it says nothing new about women. It simply admits that men have violated God's will for the human race. We need more than that. We have heard the confession. Now we need to see a firm purpose of amendment or, as Bucharest and peoples everywhere demonstrate with startling clarity, the rights of males to batter either a nation or a woman will never change.

"I became a feminist," Sally Kempton wrote, "as an alternative to becoming a masochist." It is something for all of us to think about.

Sofia

We get into Sofia, Bulgaria tomorrow morning at 8:00 a.m. I'm not sure that I can go another step, hear another cry for help, watch another woman ground under the heel of a world that does not even see her and, if it does see her, does not care about what it sees.

August 14, 1995

The whole thing just keeps getting worse: the people get dryer of spirit, the cities get duller, the hotels get less and less convenient, the meetings get less and less organized as we go. 'And all of those things are themselves learnings that no book can provide.

We arrived in Sofia a few minutes ahead of schedule, but there were no buses at the train station to take us to the Park Moksva Hotel. This bus company wasn't just "late"; this bus company didn't seem to exist at all. At least not for us. As a result, it took over two hours to get out of the station and into our rooms. The meetings were almost three hours late beginning. Then, after a brief opening session, they walked us for blocks uphill to get a public tram across the city, proud to take us to "a good restaurant for lunch." Two hundred and thirty of us on public trams. I could hardly believe the time and effort of it. And yet, the tram ride was an experience of the city that no tour bus can give. We swayed back and forth, clinging to the ceiling straps, as the tram hurled us around corners of ancient streets. The city was a dignified place, a monument to old world beauty come on hard times. Broad avenues swept around the city in exaggerated grandeur for the amount of traffic they carried. Heavy old trees lined the streets. Parks sprung up everywhere. But shop windows were sparse. Prices were high by Eastern European standards. Buildings and plazas and byways were run-down and overgrown and unpaved. There was some kind of institutional sadness here that I could not specifically identify but felt in my bones.

I have learned by this time that food is an indicator of many things here – hospitality, culture, geography and standard of living. Lunch was chilled cucumber/yogurt soup with day-old buns, a cold piece of thin, thin beef, dried up peas, hard carrots, and sticky rice, the best food they had to give us, I knew. If this is what they are able to provide for guests, I thought, what are they feeding their children? What were they eating themselves, I wondered? I had not an ounce of energy left to fight my way through the rest of the day.

We went back through the city, over huge old cobblestones, past great monuments to God-knows-what in a cab that had to be stopped in the middle of an eight-lane highway to screw a muffler back on. I held my breath and looked the other way as cars screamed by, barely making an arc around us. When, after tying the muffler to the underbelly of the chassis, the driver finally got back into the cab, he was covered with oil and mud that went from the back of his head to the back of his shoes. I could feel cultural claustrophobia in every nerve in my body. This place simply did not run – and everybody took the breakdown for granted.

We slept for three hours – in the middle of the day, something I never do. This trip is clearly demanding a type of energy I'm not used to sustaining over so long a period. But after the afternoon rest, we were ready for a nice dinner in the hotel dining room. Wine and assorted salads and spicy beef and some sort of nut cake for dessert – for two – cost about $15.00. The low prices here were as shocking as the high prices had been in Helsinki. Feeling a little guilty, I think, we gave the waiter a three-dollar tip, and he followed us, half running, all the way to the elevator, trying to carry our bags and snap open doors and say thank you, thank you, thank you. I felt guiltier than ever.

On the way upstairs again, we stopped in to see their new capitalist casino. It was on the same floor as the restaurant but it was out of a different world. A campari and soda cost $10 each. The gaming tables were empty yet in the early evening but the croupiers were as slick as anything in Atlantic City and the "girls" were all dressed up in hip high skirts and little bow ties. Clearly, somebody here has money. Somebody profited from the total breakdown of the society. Somebody was doing quite well, in fact. The only problem, I knew, is not that some are so rich; the problem is that so many are so poor.

It is sometimes hard to know which is the greater evil: Communism brought the masses rigidity and poverty and governmental controls, yes. But capitalism is bringing them gambling and pornography and poverty of the worst kind. What is really most human? What is really best for everyone? Or are both of them distortions of the human spirit in which, though we see the destructiveness of one, we refuse to admit the destructiveness of the other?

We are a caravan of eight buses now on our way to the Turkish border and a day in Istanbul. The Balkan Mountains fringe the great open fields through which we're driving, and the crops look just as rich, the fruit canning factories just as good, the cities in the background just as thriving as anything you see in the West. But they're not thriving at all. They are struggling to build an economy, to be democratic countries, to develop legal systems that guarantee the freedoms they don't know what to do with.

I don't really know how I feel about it all.

There is great potential here, but there is also a generation formed by dependence, control and a subsistence existence. "At least Communism brought us peace and food," one woman said. "At least," I thought.

"Capitalism brings war," the speaker yesterday said in assessing the situation in Yugoslavia. And another woman pointed out, "Those who made the war cannot also make the peace. They themselves are the war criminals. They can only stop the fighting." They are all points well made. They are also not that simple. After all, it was not capitalism that bred Franz Ferdinand and his assassin, a war that is still alive and well in Yugoslavia this morning, 78 years later. Capitalist gun-sellers are profiting from it, yes, but they did not make it up. What they could do, of course, is to stop enabling it. There is more than enough responsibility to go around.

All I know is that refugees streaming across borders are women, the unemployed are women, the disenfranchised are women, the battered are women, the disadvantaged are women. Everywhere. We live in a sickness of society founded upon a sickness in humanity, compounded by a sickness of the soul.

Istanbul

Istanbul was a complete surprise. It is a huge, bright, sprawling city, the cleanest I have ever seen despite its poverty, despite its invisible millions of invisible poor. There were one million people in this modern Constantinople 25 years ago. Now there are 12 million here, all come out of the mountain villages, literally thousands of them every day, to look for work, for food, for life, for a better world.

The original walls of the old city, the city of the Ottoman Turks and Crusaders, still rise majestically above the Bosporus. One Christian church stands small and mute among the many minarets where once the seat of Eastern Christendom had risen in mighty majesty. I smiled a little at the thought of me and all the little Turkish kids standing where once the Emperor Justinian with his dream of restoring the Roman Empire had strode and where the Byzantine Empire had later shaped for itself a solemn, and independent, Catholicism. How times change. Now no empire controls this fragmented little world, and the Eastern church and the Western church hold the very same Gospel, yes, but in very different ways. It is a lesson to be learned newly by everyone perhaps, even popes or potentates, who think that this world is amenable to any control that smothers culture.

In Istanbul, when our final reservations went beyond the capacity of the original hotel to meet them, we got shifted by accident to a very elegant, four-star hotel. The shift to riches was our first mistake, and like most Christians who find themselves newly rich, I failed to recognize the sin in the beauty of the temptation. It is so easy to think that all the problems of the world lie in deprivation. We forget that there are evils hidden in affluent systems as well. Now I would be able to make my e-mail connections with ease, I thought. After all, maybe everything outside the place was a little dusty, a little slow, but everything in here was Americanized to the teeth. And therein lies the tale that Marco Polo never had to tell.

The last people to get our room keys, Gail and I were the last people back to the lobby, too. The only thing that had run on time for the whole trip had just disappeared up the hill without us. Our bus was gone. We were staying here, but the opening session of the conference was scheduled for the other hotel. No one knew exactly where that was, but we did know that the conference was about to start in 15 minutes. Couldn't we take a cab? "No, no," the Turkish counter clerk said, "no reason to take a taxi. It is only 200 meters away, a ten-minute walk." Now let it be known that I do not like this fine European habit of measuring distance by time. The question is, whose ten minute pace are we talking about? Theirs or mine? But the clerk would have none of it. We would walk.

Istanbul does not function, it teems. Uphill. If the meeting site was really only 200 meters away, which I doubt, it felt like six football fields laid out end-to-end straight up. A ten-minute walk for a Chicago Bears running back maybe, but not for me.

The walk up the relentless Turkish rise wasn't easy, but it was exciting. Here we were on the streets of Istanbul, in a cauldron of strange sounds and milling crowds and endless fascinations. Turkish restaurants and Eastern music and cars careening around corners and crammed five abreast into spaces where centuries ago camel trains had walked with dignity and grace. It was hard to know whether progress had really come or gone from this place.

When we arrived at the hotel conference site, the entire delegation was still milling around in the lobby an hour after the meeting was to have begun. I was breathless and tired but bright enough to figure out that a Turkish schedule is one that gathers people early and then makes them wait. It's an interesting culture, Turkey – half Western, half Eastern. The Western part is always on time; the Eastern part waits.

But the conference was more than worth the wait. The presentation of the history of the Turkish women's movement was a brilliant synthesis of history and issues. The slightly used history teacher in me liked it a lot. On the other hand, I was most impressed by the women themselves who, in the face of Muslim fundamentalism, were confronting both religion and government at the same time. Either domain is a formidable foe. I wondered how many of them would really be able to survive the pressure of both. Two of them had already spent time in prison for their pains.

Dinner at "Pescatore's" on the Bosporus took us through Istanbul at night to the other side of town – to another continent, in fact. The trip from the side of town that was Europe to the side of town that was Asia sent a chill right up my spine. Nowhere else in the world can this happen. Nowhere else in the world is another continent simply another neighborhood. It makes you realize how fraudulent national boundaries really are.

Dinner ended with round after round of Turkish music and a dance floor of young Arab men waltzing the entire delegation. I dropped out, exhausted, but I admit I was smiling. After all, my novice mistress never mentioned the protocol for dancing Turkish dances on the Dardanelles in the midst of Turkish men. I don't think they covered that in the spirituality manuals of the time.

I waited downstairs on the waterfront for what seemed like forever, watching buses pull out one by one. Surely Gail and the rest of the dancing delegates would soon come to know the kind of exhaustion I did so we could get back to the hotel. Finally, the last hotel bus was pulling out when I raced up the steps, grabbed Gail by the wrist, and started to run for it, too exasperated to try to chase the bus and explain the problem at the same time. After all, enough is enough. "Where were you?" I asked breathlessly when we finally collapsed on the floor of the bobbing bus. "I had to pay!" she gasped. "All that wine and beer they drank at our table wasn't free! And everyone else had already left so they gave the tab to me. It took a lot of figuring in Turkish to buy my way out of there!" Poor Gail. It was a long, long table from which to inherit a bill. I should have taken that as a first warning. Everything that looks free here is not. I should also have learned from her good humor about how to deal with it all. I didn't do that either.

The next morning was what I hope will be the low point of the trip, the Waterloo of the Peace Train, the D-Day of the whole bloody excursion for me. First, I left the adaptor that powers my computer in the hotel socket – the kind of tragedy that for a writer is akin to a bus driver's dropping an ignition key down an open grate. You need it, you know where it is and you can't get it. Then, I lost my glasses, not quite as great a fiasco for someone who buys glasses at the drugstore the way I do as it would be for someone with contact lenses, I admit, but inconvenient nevertheless. Finally, and worst of all, I was charged $91.00 for 18 attempted Compuserve calls that never worked! In fact, the clerk followed me onto the bus, waving the charge slips and furious. How could I possibly owe for what I did not get? And then, to put a fine point on the whole transaction, the Saracen gave me the $9.00 change from my traveler's check in Turkish money. And I was on my way out of Turkey! My only satisfaction of the entire day was tearing the bill in half like play money from a Monopoly game. Take that, Sultan Somebody. I am not afraid of your curved little scimitars, so there! And then I bent over and picked it up and put it back together again and donated it to the women's shelter. Easy, Joan, easy.

If truth were known, I was sad to leave Istanbul. It is a city full of mystery from the East and excitement from the West.

Istanbul

There were things I expected to see in Istanbul: women in chadors, minarets in profusion, money scams in the airport, vendors everywhere. And I was not disappointed. Village women swept by fully veiled, trailing a wake of small children. Muezzin competed with trams and trains and the sound of a thousand car horns for sacred attention in a secular world. A woman on our train accepted the offer of 120 United States dollars in return for her own hundred-dollar bill — and then discovered moments later that somehow she had been deftly separated from the second $120 as well. Street after street bulged with small stores and tabletop bazaars. Television and travel agencies had done their work on me well.

At the same time, there were also things I did not expect to see in Istanbul, things for which I had not been nearly so well prepared: gleaming new office buildings, meticulously clean streets and two types of tombstones. The first kind of tombstone marker, a small obelisk topped by a circle of cement, has a "head" on it. The second kind of marker does not. Under the first, the one with the head, they tell us, lie the men. Under the second — the headless ones — lie women. The symbols were all too graphic, all too poignantly true.

"Turkey," the speaker told us, "is caught between two worlds." This city built on two continents, the city of two traditions — Christian Constantinople and Muslim Istanbul — symbolizes like few others in the world, perhaps, the condition of cultures everywhere. Everywhere, women are treated as if they have no brains, but women are beginning to rise from their tombs of insignificance and demand the resurrection of human rights. At least in Turkey.

A sign at "The Purple Roof," a center for battered women off a mud alley in the center of the city, reads "Women's Rights Are Human Rights." I've been thinking about that ever since we boarded the train to return to our comfortable little worlds away from state-supported religious fundamentalism, away from village traditions and city discrimination, away from the repressions of women's human rights said to be good, said to be godly and, therefore, said to be unchangeable. As if the God who created humanity to begin with, created half of it to be the domestic chattel of the other.

"A right," former Attorney General Ramsey Clark said, "is not what someone gives you; it's what no one can take from you." Tell that to women. Better yet, tell that to men about women.

The Turkish women's movement links the two with disturbing clarity.

If the right to dissent is a basic human right, Turkish women point out, women do not have it. In Turkish law, the man is still defined as "the head of the family." It is the man whose views prevail in case of dispute, who determines domicile, who represents the family to third parties. It is the man who makes business decisions for the family, even if the woman is an economics major. It is the man who determines the place of the family home, even if being there isolates the woman or makes education impossible for the girl children. It is the man whose ideas prevail, even when those ideas are limited, even when those ideas are wrong.

If the right to own property is a basic human right, Turkish women insist, women do not have it. In case of divorce, for instance, though women are said in Turkish constitutional law to to be equal, all "immovable property," all real estate, land and related items — the curtains, the silverware, the rugs, for instance — are registered in his name and belong to him. What she gets from divorce, in other words, is the right to take her children and live on the streets — unless, of course, he gets the children, too. Legislation designed to change this is pending in the Turkish parliament at this time but, the women told us, "All men are against this," and the women doubt that it will pass. "You should never marry when you are in love," a Swedish doctor advised the group. "You will trust too much. Be sure to make a good business arrangement." The point, of course, is that men apparently do not love women enough to love them justly.

If the right to life is a basic human right, Turkish women make us realize, women do not have it. Violence against women rages, an invisible sin, a silent one. The police do not listen to women, the government does not supply shelters, the courts do not protect her. In the end, they send her back to the family "where she belongs," and she goes because she won't be "safe" anyplace else.

Rape is a tool of torture in Turkish prisons. There is no such thing as rape in marriage. The property of men, women are evaluated according to their value to men. Violence against women, therefore, is punished according to the value that a violated women has to a man. If a man kidnaps a married woman or mother, he will receive a greater punishment than if he kidnaps an unmarried woman. If he rapes a virgin, it is more serious than if she is not. If he abuses a prostitute, his sentence will be reduced by one-third. Adultery is a crime for both men and women, but for her it consists of a single act. For a man to be accused of adultery, he must be living with the woman for at least six months or have had a liaison with her in the family home itself. Boys will be boys, you know.

And under it all, though education is both compulsory and free in Turkey, one-third of the women are illiterate because male magistrates and civic officials understand why men don't send daughters to school.

Istanbul, this world of two continents, two cities, two traditions is locked in mortal battle with itself. Westernism touches every aspect of life, and fundamentalism rages when it fails. People from the villages find themselves in frightening territory and turn to the only stability they know – custom. Young women wear chadors to be safe on the streets, not necessarily because they espouse them for religious reasons. Illiteracy serves to mask even the existence of paltry laws on behalf of women.

But though law is an instrument of liberation, it is not a guarantee of it. Women on the Peace Train remembered aloud, in the face of the Turkish situation, women in the United States itself who are beaten regularly, left without financial security, blocked in their career ambitions, denied access to decision-making levels of management, professional bodies and government – all because they are women. Then the problem gets even murkier. Then, an Irish family therapist reminded the group, the real questions must be asked: If women are educated, if the law requires equal treatment and if little changes despite it, is the problem inside women themselves? Have women so internalized the gender roles, the traditions, the religious definitions, the social norms, the public standards, that they themselves cannot bear the vilification, the rejection, the amount of negative evaluation, the marginalization it will take to change their own lives where it counts, in the personal arena?

It's not a pleasant conversation but it may be a necessary one if what started out to be a liberation movement is ever to liberate women from themselves.

"Elder," the seeker said. "How can I ever become freed?" And the Holy One answered, "Who has ever put you in bondage?"

Next time, Kazahkstan. In the meantime, keep talking about such things. One thing I am learning here for sure is that all the women in the world depend on it.

The Ukraine

August 16, 1995

Today was a wonderful lost day spent rambling through the Ukrainian countryside, past gypsy caravans and horse carts, along strings of soft haycocks and acres of sunflowers. No meetings, no buses, no language problems. The daily schedule of lectures and discussion groups proceed regardless here on the train, of course, but they are not meetings in the formal sense of the word. They are more in the style of teach-ins, and they have welded the train into one large think tank. Those who do go take notes and then teach them again in the cabins at night to the people who did not go that day.

So the train is a hive of activity. People sway up and down the cars, back and forth, in one unending stream from morning to night. I have bruises on every part of my body from lurching against walls and jumping over car locks from wagon to wagon in the attempt to meet this person, talk to that one, interview this one, check information with that one. I used to think that learning was an intellectual activity. I have found out that here it takes every ounce of physical stamina you have just to get through the day. Don't think for a moment that 25 days on a train is 25 days in a deck chair.

We are on our way back to Odessa. I was glad to be able to stay on the train for a change, to have a little quiet, a modicum of privacy, some time to think.

I wrote the article on Istanbul and then spent the better part of the rest of the day trying to get it printed out so that I can at least send it as a fax if I can't get on-line in Odessa. We won't be there very long, so I can't take a lot of time trying. Besides that, after spending $100 in Turkey on false attempts, I am mightily burned by the whole process. And pretty close to broke, as well.

It has been almost impossible to change money along the way. In the first place, it's a terrible waste. We're not in any place long enough to spend what we change, which leaves us with a lot of unused money that no one wants to change back into anything else later. And secondly, they don't really want their money. They want ours. We have oiled our way across Eastern Europe on a pocket full of US one-dollar bills. And we are running out of them. So much for that great old American Express motto: "Don't leave home without it." The fact is that credit cards haven't done us a whole lot of good at all. Right now I would prefer a piggy bank to a Gold Card.

Convenience is not a characteristic of Eastern Europe. Life on the train has been a series of border crossings and middle of the night passport checks and hours of wheel-changing. Yesterday they did it again. They pumped the whole car up on hydraulic lifts, disengaged the wheel base, ran a new set of wheels under the body of the train the way you change wheels on a car and then let us down on them again. It is a process that either leaves you standing on the platform in the hot sun or suspended in mid-air in a humid, airless wagon for hours. The first time it happened it was 4:00 a.m. and I slept through it. Yesterday it was in the heat of the afternoon, and I was caught 15 feet up in the air trying to get Brunn and Ian's printer to work. They are fine people, gentle and generous, who have probably saved this whole trip for me – and maybe for the entire press corps as well. Without them and their printer, I don't know how I could possibly have made every deadline once the e-mail stopped working. Ian has managed to plait and paste wires together for every switch on the train. I just follow the extension cords and there he is, trying to make it possible for the rest of us to put out press releases and stories about women that the world press is steadfastly ignoring. He doesn't seem deterred. He wears a button that says "Men of quality are not threatened by women of equality." I have never seen a better demonstration of the idea in anyone than I have in him.

During the wheel-changing, everybody else got off to walk the fields or have picnics with the food they pilfered from the dining car or bought from old women on railroad platforms. I held on to the open doorway of the wagon and watched them loll around the fields like figures in an early American farm scene. I tell myself I'm still in the 20th century, but I'm not sure.

Everyone on the train is friendly, and they go from car to car and talk all day long, getting to know new people and learning new things. I would have done that at one point in my life. At this point, however, I have had years of community and feel a

great desire to simply be alone for a change or to talk more
deeply with a few people rather than to be introduced to many.
And we are surrounded by wonderful women: Audley is a harp-
sichordist from Australia with a soul as broad as her education.
Midi is a long-time Peacelinks member from Pittsburgh, whose
wisdom and presence brings peace wherever she goes. Dolores is
a neonatologist from Texas, who is as funny as she is strong.
Agnes Anne is a Methodist Deaconess, with the kind of goodness
that defies the human condition. Midge is a sculptor, full of life
and as generous as the heart of God. Marion and Marilyn are
mother and daughter who genuinely like one another and are
gentle presence to everyone else as well. Dorothy is an elderly
woman who spent five years in a Japanese concentration camp in
Manila during World War II and seeks peace with all her life.
Anne is a cultured woman with a quiet smile who has the gift of
listening and loving whatever you say. There are young women in
this wagon, as well – Barbara from Switzerland and Maria from
Germany – who work with the disadvantaged and carry their burdens in their own hearts. And Ruth, the Unitarian psychologist,
and Mim, the Quaker-become-Methodist, keep the conversations
going and the group a group, from one end of the wagon to the
other. Gail takes pictures and I write. In between times, we tell
jokes and outrageous stories and start serious conversations designed to make everybody think outside the boxes of our lives.
It's a nice group, a thoughtful group, a pleasant group to be with.
Gone are the days when all those differences would have been
barriers to good conversations. On the contrary, they have deep-
ened them by layers, enriched them beyond measure.

Every evening the day's wash goes out on the banisters in the
corridor. Every morning, the day's route gets sketched on Dolores'
wall map of Eastern Europe. Every day someone reads out loud to
the rest of us what the guidebooks have to say about the areas
we're traveling through. I smile at that. We can't see a thing but
we tell ourselves we can.

We will be in Odessa in a couple of hours but it will be a
very short visit, from about 10:00 in the morning until 10:00 at
night, when we will get back on the train for Kazakhstan. To tell
the truth, I am much more interested in getting mail from home
right now than I am in being greeted on one more platform in
one more country.

Odessa

The nice thing about this trip is that the unplanned has become the predictable. It is not, as we expected, a "short" visit to Odessa. We have literally not been allowed to leave. The word is that the Chinese do not want us to cross over into China before August 26, though we are scheduled to be there the 23rd. The rumor/speculation is that the Chinese do not want us in the region near Lop Nor, where they have just recently exploded their atomic bomb. Whatever the real agenda, they put pressure on the Russians, who are running the train, who put pressure on the Ukrainians, who are in charge of the local program to keep us here. And here we are. Welcome to the totalitarian state.

The whole railroad station was closed to mark our arrival yesterday. The red-coated brass band was there and hundreds and hundreds of people. It gave a little new energy to this group of straggling pilgrims for whom greetings and buses have become boringly the same. But the energy didn't last for long.

The "Hotel Victoria" is, at best, shelter for the night. It is not a hotel in any common meaning of the word. It is certainly the poorest of any hotel that we have had so far anywhere. Whatever you expect in a hotel they do not have. Including water. Which is not to say that the hospitality here isn't deeply moving, genuinely outpouring, gloriously real. It is just that they have very little to give. It is just that the facilities cannot possibly meet the level of care the people set out to provide. The city, for instance, turned the hot water on for one hour to mark our arrival, a generous and sensitive gesture. "So you can all have a warm bath," the hostess said with smiling pride. But though we all "showered," none of us got much water to do it with. What water there was, was cold and that simply a trickle – whatever their attempts to skirt the austerity regime of the city in our behalf. Yet, wonderful smiling women met every one of us separately, conducted us to our rooms, gave us nice fresh towels for the showers most of us couldn't take and hovered about in the halls to meet our every need. It's a pathetic place, meaning "full of pathos," sad in a happy kind of way and happy in a sad kind of way.

Intent on getting my most recent article to the *National Catholic Reporter* on time, I went by cab across town to the Hotel London with Gail and Angela Dometsch, Colombian president of the International Federation of Women Lawyers, who were also sending reports back to their respective countries. The Hotel London had everything that our hotel lacked. I was glad to see the place, just to know that the country was capable of supporting adequate accommodations. I couldn't help but wonder, however, who really used the place – and for what. If it wasn't tourists and travelers like us, who was it?

The faxes went through easily, they charged us $3.00 a page and I felt quite satisfied with the whole process. Gail, on the other hand, had quite an afternoon of it. She must have sent her article 25 times but the line was always busy. When, in desperation, she finally called *The Irish Times* again to say that she couldn't get through, they discovered that their fax machine was out of paper. She called it "a real Irish story." I laughed every time I thought about it. So much for Irish news about an earthquake in Japan if the Irish fax machine is out of paper. I remembered all those Irish stories my Irish family told about Irish imperturbability and I loved them more than ever.

Best of all about the trip, however, was the fact that even though it had taken hours to complete a 15-minute process, we were only a matter of blocks away from the Opera House where they had planned a night of entertainment for the group with "The Renaissance Ballet of Moscow." The Ukrainians, after all, had a trainload of women on their hands. What were they supposed to do with us? Somebody had to dream up something to keep us occupied. And who, I wondered, was paying the bill for a stopover the trainload did not plan and did not want to make? Not us, I bet. Anyway, since we were in the area, we could go there and see if we could still get in for any part of the show.

Just because we were close to the Opera House, however, does not mean that maneuvering the rest of the day wasn't complex. We had run out of small dollar bills sending the faxes. We walked the streets from office to office but no money changer would give us a penny. We hadn't had anything to eat. And, most conclusive of all, we didn't have any small money left – which meant that if we decided to go straight back to the hotel we would have to give a cab driver a large bill and kiss goodbye any hope of getting change. A $50 cab ride was not my idea of a good day. So, the solution seemed to be to walk as far as the Opera House, see what was left of the ballet, and take one of our own tour buses back to the hotel with the rest of the group. It all seemed so sensible, so fortuitous. When we got to the park, however, sitting out in the open air and watching local teenagers give "pony rides" on unsaddled full-grown horses to small children seemed to be a lot better choice than sitting one more hour in an auditorium chair, however much I like ballet. And it wasn't a bad plan at all till I interrupted it. No, actually, I scuttled it.

There, in the middle of the biggest plaza in Odessa, right in front of the Opera House and in full view of God and everybody at the intermission, I threw up on the Opera House lawn. The gastroenteritis that had plagued the train for several days hit me full force in the middle of town. Without warning. Without Kleenex. Without an ounce of dignity. Let's think of a comparable situation to make clear the ambience: Kennedy Center, maybe. The Metropolitan Opera, perhaps. The Rotunda of the Capitol in Washington, D.C., possibly. On second thought, let's not think of comparable situations. It is more than I can bear. With little in the way of options, I pulled myself together – whatever that meant – and went into the Opera to be close to a lavy, to wait for a bus. It was not one of the more cultural experiences of my life. But it taught me a lot, nevertheless: It taught me that dignity does not depend on never getting into embarrassing situations. It depends on getting out of them with poise. It taught me that there is always more endurance in us than we think there is. It taught me that Eastern Europeans are very cultured people.

I sat in the back of the gold-gilded Opera House and, despite my own difficulty with trying to concentrate on the show, marveled at the enthusiasm of the audience. The theater was packed in that wonderful part of the day that Europeans love so well, the time just after the close of the business day and just before the beginning of the supper hour, when droves of them stop at local theaters for concerts and symphonies and ballet productions on their way home from work. Young and old swayed in their seats, clapped to the music and shouted with approval for the dancers and the traditional presentation of bouquets to the stars of the show. Then, Ukrainians in shirt-sleeves and business suits, in long dresses and simple ones, strolled home for supper with little money in their pockets, perhaps, but with quality in their souls. It is a strange contrast, this love of culture with a history of totalitarianism. Maybe it is precisely the love of beauty that saved Eastern Europe from the stultifying effects of centralized mindlessness.

It was a long night. I had never realized before how hard it is to have a sick stomach in a place where you cannot drink the water and there are neither towels nor paper to wash with, but I got through. The floor woman brought a cup of strong, black tea. Women from the train dug down deep in travel bags and got me a collection of medicines designed to cure stomachs of every ailment known to humankind. Gail went for Coke – and came back with ginger ale, the only soda the hotel had to offer that night. I slept on a mattress on the floor to be near the open door and to survive the stifling heat, to avoid the broken wires in the bed frame, to be able to move as fast as possible when I got sick again. Funny the things we take for granted, funny the things we do not realize in this world, funny how far away from the basics we live and never even know it.

I am now back with the group in an auditorium in Odessa. It is impossible to stay in the hotel – though the organizers tried to make that arrangement for several of us – because no one knows when we will be leaving Odessa or from what point at the station. We are all sitting politely, listening to more protocol presentations, but actually people are far more interested now in what is going on in China than in what is going on in Odessa. I can hardly concentrate on either. I am clinging to the little that is left in me of equilibrium and good humor and waiting to get back on the train. Dying from gastroenteritis in an auditorium in Odessa is not my idea of a glorious death, but the way I feel right now, it would be welcome.

A young black American woman gave a "speech" during the session (called later a "diatribe" by many here) that, true as it may be about American racism, was perhaps politically out of kilter, inappropriate some said, in this setting. I wasn't offended by it. In fact, everything in it is true. It's just that it sounded more as if it should be being said to Americans than to Europeans. The subject of the session, after all, at least according to the program, was "Peace around the Black Sea." If she made a connection between the two subjects, it was apparently lost on many.

At the same time, harsh and unnecessarily confrontative as it seemed to many, I'm sure that as women we often do the same thing to men. It is such a delicate situation. How else do the oppressed express themselves? How else do they get heard unless they jar us out of our comfortable reveries? Who else will listen to us often, to our anger, to our exasperation, to our frustration, except our friends?. And at the same time, how many times can you beat up on your allies and expect them to maintain their love and their support for us? "These young people just do not know who their friends are," women said who had demonstrated in Washington, worked on Dr. King's campaigns and hired the first minorities for white jobs at white salary levels. I thought of the 30 years of my own life spent speaking for the oppressed and wondered, looking at these young women, how often we all destroy our companions on the journey to justice in the name of protest. And yet how necessary the protest is. Maybe losing our friends and loved ones over issues is what, in the end, integrity really comes down to in all our private little lives. Painful as the thought of that is.

After a group meeting full of more formalities, more speeches, more heat, and less attention, we were rounded up into buses again and taken from place to place – a Russian kindergarten, a "peace park" full of the weapons the Ukrainians had used to repel the Germans during the siege of Odessa, the Potemkin Steps where the first phase of the Russian Revolution was put down. The field trip taught us a great deal. The school, for instance, was a residential center for children whose parents were in prison, a concept our own society could well afford to explore. At the same time, it was all busy-work designed to keep us occupied. After all, we still couldn't go anyplace and we had no hotel rooms in which to wait. So we were getting the tour of the city while the organizers were "negotiating" with the Chinese. If you believe that, I've got a bridge I want to sell you. I am getting the distinct impression that no one "negotiates" with the Chinese. You simply delay the inevitable.

I was half sick, very hot and restless. I could feel the agitation of being taken from place to place begin to grate like sandpaper in the center of my soul. I simply wanted to get back to the train. At the same time, I couldn't help being impressed and grateful for the general good nature of the group. Representatives from every country in the delegation, Gail among them, were off to one place or another sending 42 faxes to 42 State Departments to appraise our separate countries of what was happening to us and to ask for diplomatic intervention. In the meantime, the rest of us simply followed our Ukrainian hosts back and forth from monument to monument, sure that things would get cleared up any moment now. We had, after all, planned this trip months ago, the route and timetable had been agreed to by the Chinese, and we had paid our money – a Western clincher if ever there was one. We were more than willing to talk about it, of course, clear up any misunderstandings that had apparently occurred, but then we wanted to be out of here and on our way. As planned.

I began to realize that however polite and positive everyone else was being about the situation, at least on the surface, at the level of personal reaction, I was deeply troubled about the re-scheduling of the train and the lack of communication that went with it. The American in me was beginning to erupt with a passion. The whole notion of being made to stay in a place we wanted out of by people we did not see and could not talk to gave me an insight into the vagaries, the violence of totalitarianism. We were pawns in a game that had no players. We simply could not find the person responsible for this situation nor could we get the problem defined. They just did not want us to come into China on the day originally determined. No reason given, no explanations accepted. We were stranded. And, we learned via the grapevine, not only were we left to our own devices in Eastern Europe, they wanted us to pay extra for the privilege! In my country, that is called extortion.

Then, the Chinese government talked to the Ukrainian government who talked to the Russian government that runs the trains who talked to the local organizers in Odessa who told us when we got here that we were to stay here. The Russians and Ukrainians were simply not prepared to send off one of their trains to a border that was closed to them and so be responsible for a train-load of women from 42 countries stuck in territory where we did not want to be but were not permitted to leave. They couldn't, after all, just put us off the train at the border and leave us there without housing and without food for two days. On the other hand, they could not take us into Chinese territory without the permission of the Chinese government. Not without risking an international incident one way or the other. They were stuck and so were we. The whole thing was simply out of our hands. We waited for help from on high, wherever that was. But no help came. We were, after all, only a trainload of women.

August 22, 1995

We left Odessa at about 10:30 p.m. on August 18. We were a somber but amiable group. People pored over maps, trying to figure out where we were being taken. I was worrying about meeting the next transmission deadline in Urumchi. If it was true that we were not permitted to stop there, then I would have no way to both write and send the Alma-Ata piece from Alma-Ata in the same day. Which left me only one choice. I could write an article about the train itself, the very thing the US State Department bulletin warned writers against, and send it instead. To criticize the Chinese government, the bulletin informed us, is a felony in China for which a journalist can be either jailed or deported. I made up my mind to write it anyway. What is the use of being a writer if you don't tell the truth? On the other hand, come to think about it, what is the use of being a writer if you do?

At about midnight, after we were almost as far north as Moscow again, we began to wonder if they had changed routes on us altogether and were about to send us over the Northern route through the Trans-Siberian sector of Russia. That route would shunt us down through Mongolia and surely slow the trip even more. We began to wonder if we would get to Beijing even in time for the opening of the conference, let alone a day early. But, at about midnight, the train turned east again and we realized that we were traveling according to plan. Hopes rose. Maybe there had been some diplomatic intervention someplace. But no. In fact, the plans were far more complex than that. We had not only been put out of Odessa late, but we were now being sent off for two full days on the train through endless countryside on the way to nowhere. Or at least to nowhere we knew about or had ever planned to go. I found myself humming a song I'd learned as a child about a guy named Charlie and the Boston subway system. I sang: "Oh, did he ever return? No, he never returned. And his fate is still unlearned. He will ride forever 'neath the streets of Boston, on the train that never returned." Or something like that. I used to think that song was funny. I was now finding it a little ominous.

Voronezh/Saratov

After two nights and a day and a half on the train, we stopped, finally, in a Russian city called Voronezh. We were there, they told us, for eight hours. We got in at about noon. The train, they said, would be back in the station at about 8:50 pm. We were on our own. See ya' around, Charlie.

Voronezh had been "a closed city" – one of those secret Soviet cities that created some of the world's deadliest nuclear technology – until the end of the Cold War. Closed cities were actually taken off maps, closed both to incoming and outgoing traffic, devoid of visitors – even the relatives of people who lived there – completely sealed off from the rest of the Soviet Union because of the nature of the high-secret industries located there. Now, faced with crippling cuts in the military budget, cities full of scientists, technicians and nuclear physicists are left trying desperately to develop new industries. At recent Russian trade fairs, the Associated Press reported, once-prestigious weapons' designers exhibited leather goods, herbal medicines, bathroom fixtures, and ceramic pigs in bonnets.

Voronezh was a dirty, grubby, poor, inartistic little place – just like all the rest of the old Iron Curtain cities we'd seen along the route. We wandered through the little shops around the station. I've never been in more pitiable circumstances. Haiti is desperate and the Philippines are swollen with the poor. But Voronezh was pitiable. Here were proud people trying to look as if nothing had changed in life and everything had changed for them, their country, their work, their livelihood, their standard of living, even their philosophy of government. Who were they now? And why? What was left for them to believe in? What was left for them to do?

When I went to the Soviet Union as a member of past delegations, we had been concentrated in major cities and restricted to shopping in the *Beriozkas* – except for a quick trip through "Gum Department Store" in Red Square. "Gum" was a disorganized and jumbled mess of a place by Western department store designs, yes, but it seemed at least to have the kind of bustle and life and categories of things that average shopping centers do. Here, we saw the real Russia. Every store was dark and sparse. Every shop sold the same things: the same commercial brands – most of them English, in fact – the same items, the same foods we were eating on the train. Dried up tomatoes, scrawny cucumbers, bland white cheeses were everywhere. The vegetable "market" in a small shop was a bin or two of old lettuce, wrinkled carrots, dried-up mushrooms. The fruit they were selling on the street corners was bruised and spotted. There was nothing here to buy – except cigarettes and liquor. Cigarettes and liquor stands were everywhere, invitations to dull the senses in a society where there is little else to comfort them.

In the center of the city stood a large monument, an obelisk of either atoms or of planets, I never did figure out which. At any rate, there was no doubt why the city had been closed. Voronezh's claim to fame was that it had obviously harbored a center for nuclear research or rocket development programs. There are still soldiers everywhere there, more in fact than we had seen in St. Petersburg. They all look quite harmless now, compared to the menacing precision I'd seen in Moscow years before. They were jostling around in khakis and hanging out of old trucks. They stood in groups laughing and joking or kind of loped along, briefcases in hand, to offices, I presumed. Open-faced blond boys, most of them. Tired-looking old men with overhanging bellies, some of them. No spit and polish, here. No menacing looks. Nothing certainly to be afraid of at all. Funny how the face of the enemy can change when it is no longer an enemy.

If anything struck me at all, it was the total isolation of the place. I had just never heard of anyone closing an entire city before – at least not since the Middle Ages. And the claustral living had clearly affected everyone from young to old. People here are still curious about strangers as a result of their years of isolation, and we were more of an event to them than they were to us. Small children turned in the street and stared. Men and boys bunched together and stretched their heads over one another's shoulders to watch us pass. Women in babushkas and long black skirts or upswept hairdos and old spike heels smiled at us from afar or sat and looked at us in our slacks and jackets, backpacks and Peace Train T-shirts, Reeboks and sunglasses with barely veiled interest. I got the impression that one generation of women was staring another one right in the face.

At 6:30 the Peace Train group gathered in the city's central park for a meeting – one of those encounter group sessions where people talk about their feelings. This time the feelings were about racism – the kind being felt by younger people of color on the train, and the kind felt by nationals who resented the presence of so many Americans on the train.

The perceived racism I thought might be accounted for, at least in part, as much a function of the age gap as it was of prejudice. The older women listened with concern and with disbelief. These are the women who marched in Selma and resisted the Vietnam War and stood with the Rainbow Coalition. A number of them turned away hurt. But the conversation was an exercise in self-determination and it was healthy. It just happened to be a strange audience for it. "This morning," one of the young women said, "I was called Samira for the third time in a row. Look at my face. Learn my name. We do not 'all look alike.'" I stopped myself from smiling. I wondered if the women who called her Samira remembered anybody's names anymore, including their own nieces and nephews. God help me if they give us a name-recognition test before they let us leave the train. I may never be heard from again.

The anti-Americanism they talked about I attributed to the suffocation people feel – even Europeans – from American businesses, American products, and American power everywhere. I felt the resentment in Rome in 1972 and I felt it here this week. It has something to do with "bearing the sins of the fathers."

I waited for the train with new respect for the children of Israel who yearned for the fleshpots of Egypt. It is easy, when things are hard, when things don't get better faster, to turn against the very people who led you out of even worse conditions.

Yesterday they put us off the train in Saratov, another historically closed city, to waste a little more time. Ruth and Gail and I walked the streets for blocks, looking for something that looked interesting. The scene was much the same as it had been in Voronezh: bare store shelves, cheap goods, dirty streets and a crumble-down station in a rebuilt city. Thrown up after the devastation of World War II, it was already collapsing. But the Russians on the street seemed unaware of the situation, impassive, inured to it all.

This time I was a little more prepared for the day than I had been in Voronezh, however. I had sweet-talked the stewards into

changing a $5.00 bill into Russian rubles for me. This time we
cleaned up. By the time we got back to the train, we had 4
apples, 6 oranges, one package of dates, a big hunk of good
cheese, a round loaf of fresh bread and two bottles of Coke.
Price: $4.50. Wherever they were taking us next, we were ready.

Eventually Ruth went off with a group on the way to the
riverfront to find a Volga boatman. I calculated the distance and
decided that collecting rivers was not my passion in life. Gail and
I sat in the park and played chess in the sun. We watched one
derelict roll another, pushed off a local panhandler, and chased
the sun from park bench to park bench. In the end, we left the
park with our egos intact. The game score was now 2 wins-2
losses each.

Back on the train – home – we told the stories of the day and
drank hot tea out of Russian samovar cups and went from cabin
to cabin, checking in, comparing experiences, swapping dates for
bananas, and most of all tying bits and pieces of information together to make sense of where we were and where we were
going and what we did and didn't know. The public address announcements that have been part of every day of train life to this
point are getting fewer and further between now. The point is that
not even the organizers, apparently, know much about what is
going to happen to us next. We are even out of range now of our
one tie to the outside world – the BBC Broadcasts which have
been being relayed down the train PA system to us every day by
the woman who owns the lone shortwave radio on the train.
Eventually everyone settled into cabins, not much smarter than
they had been before we left. I went on reading Anne Tyler's
Accidental Tourist. It's a good book, but I must admit that I do
not find it gripping. But right now a book that is "gripping" is the
least of my needs. The book is in English, and that is more than
enough. Every little bit of normalcy counts these days.

Change of Plans

The Chinese invented chess, they tell me, and, having become a pawn in their game, I now believe it. Before we left the United States, there were people who questioned the very idea of choosing China as a site for a Conference on Women: China, where women have historically been buried alive at birth, crippled into subservience, used as property. They may have been more right that we knew.

This is an article that few Americans expect to read and fewer expect to write. This week's column should be on the condition of women in Kazakhstan, the next scheduled stop on the Peace Train route. But I can't count on writing it because I can't count on getting there to find out what it's like for women in that part of the world. What's more, even if I get to Alma-Ata, Kazakhstan, I will certainly not get to stop in Urumchi, China, the border town from which I had intended to transmit this article.

The fact is that I don't know right now what life is like for those Kazakhstani women, and I may never find out. All I know is what it is like for the women on this Peace Train at this moment — and that is controlled, confused and uncertain.

The situation begs for explanation. Instead of going to Alma-Ata as we should, we are now riding around Russia on a 16-car train because we are not permitted to leave this country and no one has a good reason why.

It happened like this. When we arrived for our scheduled 10-hour stop in Odessa, we discovered that our plans — long-scheduled and jointly agreed to by the Peace Train organizing committee, the travel agency and the Chinese government — had been changed, without our knowledge and without our consent. We were not permitted to leave Odessa in the evening as arranged, we were told. The Chinese had determined that we had to wait until August 26 to pass into China instead of on August 24, as they had once assented to, and that we could not stop in Urumchi at any time. We could, in other words, go to Beijing but we could not stop anywhere, see anyone, talk to any Chinese women on the way, whatever our program, whatever our previous arrangements.

Peace Train organizers sent faxes to officials and Foreign Ministers in 42 countries that read,

> We write on behalf of the WILPF Peace Train traveling from Helsinki to Beijing for the UN Fourth World Conference on Women.

> We are in Odessa and facing problems continuing our journey. Our plan, until this point, has been to arrive in Alma-Ata on August 22 and

cross the border to China on the 24th. The schedule had included one stop in China at Urumchi before reaching Beijing. The Chinese welcomed and invited the Peace Train. They had agreed to the details. The travel agency and the train authorities have been obliged by the Chinese government to change our China border crossing to two days later, to take a more expensive, fast train for three days to Beijing, and to eliminate the Urumchi stop.

The additional cost we are not able or willing to pay. We are an NGO without money and the participants cannot pay this additional cost.

We ask you to contact the Chinese embassy in your country requesting authorities to use their good offices to help in this situation. . . .

But so far, no help has come.

The whole notion of being made to stay in a place we wanted to be out of, by people we did not see and could not talk to, gave me an insight into the vagaries, the violence of totalitarianism. Somewhere, someone had decided that, for no discernible reason whatsoever, we could not cross the border at the time we planned and must wait for the time they planned. Then that government talked to the Ukrainian government, who talked to the Russian government that runs the trains, who talked to the local or-

ganizers in Odessa, who told us when we got here that we were not able to leave. It was a delicate situation: the Russians and Ukrainians were simply not willing to send a train to a border that is closed to it and risk an international incident. Nor did they want to be responsible for a trainload of people from 42 nations stranded in their territory. So, they are driving us around Russia, slowly, killing time until we are allowed to enter China.

It is an experience that not many Americans have ever had. It brings a feeling of powerlessness, of helplessness, of human insignificance, of betrayal by the people who, having finally issued visas, were now willy-nilly revoking the terms of them. It is, at the same time, an experience common to many people around this world — even at our own borders — and to most women everywhere who are controlled by things they do not see and do not have the power, the resources, or the freedom to change.

The Peace Train has now, oddly enough, become a metaphor for women everywhere who, on their way to a better world, are stopped and blocked and obstructed along the road by people who know better for them, who never bother to talk to them about it, who swoop down and take charge of their lives. Every woman reformer in history has known such ridicule and trivialization and obstruction — Elizabeth Cady Stanton, Lucretia Mott, Margaret Sanger, Eleanor Roosevelt and Betty Friedan, but they went on. And so are we. But why? Why do women persist in their demands for equality when they are left in absolutely no doubt how unacceptable it is? I asked that question of women from every continent on this train. The answers never wavered:

"Because it is right," American Theresa Wilson, Peace Links' Vice-President for International Programs, said.

"To make life better for other women whose lives are even worse than our own," Anchalee Chaiwdraporn, the journalist from Thailand said.

"Because equality is one small step toward changing society to a new feminist world view — a world beyond a culture of competition, of domination, and of war. You can't influence the system without it," Barbara Lochbiller, secretary general of the Woman's International League for Peace and Freedom in Geneva said.

"Because the 21st century will be the century of the empowerment of women and therefore a century of peace," Angela Dolmetsch, treasurer of the International Federation of Women Lawyers said.

"To create a new society," Marilyn Clemens, director of WILPF, USA said. "We have no other choice."

"Because we cannot have peace without equality," Indian Dr. Krishna Ahooja Palel from the Women's World Summit Foundation in Geneva said.

"Because rights are not given; they must be taken," Tayba Sherif, a Sudanese member of the UN High Commission for Refugees, said.

"The journey of a thousand miles," the Chinese Lao-Tzu says, "starts from beneath one's feet." No doubt about it: chess game or no chess game, this train is still going "to Beijing and beyond." Let the Chinese know that women are not easily put in check. Even if it means, as we have, going an extra thousand miles.

Alma-Ata

Sometime during the night we crossed the border into Kazakhstan and woke up this morning to wide-open skies and vast, empty plains that stretched as far as the eye could see. It was a welcome break from the highgrass villages and dour, drab cities we'd been seeing for so long. The journey from Helsinki to Petersburg to Kiev to Bucharest to Sofia to Istanbul to Odessa – and then all the way back up the same route nearly to Moscow – had been an unending stretch of old, dark, wooden villages. Now at least, there was sun and blue skies and a feeling of openness.

I am a cacophony of images these days. No matter where I am when I close my eyes, I see a train bed too narrow to allow me to pull my legs up for fear of tilting over the side of the bunk; a dank, dark little store in Saratov that sold calculators and then toted up the bill on an abacus; a train asea in a corridor of women's wash lines; a dining car breakfast table full of greasy salami and sweating cheese and porridge without milk; one long, unending valley of group gardens; small fields full of soft haystacks, field workers strung across vast plains, and string after string of wooden villages marked by corrugated roofs and desultory people almost completely devoid of style or color. They eked a living out of these tight little places, cultivated their gardens to the edge of their fences, and had children who watched the train go by with an intensity in their eyes and a set to their jaws that was enough to break open the heart of the world. What would the future be like for them? How was it possible that we all lived the same world, they and we? We with our televisions and computers; they with their bicycles and donkey carts.

This trip provides more experience than excitement. If by excitement we mean variety and glitz and frenetic activity, this is not it. No, on this trip the excitement goes far deeper than that. The excitement of this trip is being able to see and touch and hear for ourselves what nothing in our own antiseptic world prepares us to know about life here, about life for the rest of the world, about life that is lived out of the soul instead of out of a package. The experience of endurance itself – of enduring the empty shelves, the interminable waits, the broken-down machinery, the dry water pipes, the warm drinks and cold food – the experience of coming to understand the world from the vantage point of limitation, a condition few American minds can even conjure up, let alone take for granted, underlies it all. This is the kind of excitement this trip offers. This is the kind of excitement that excitement is all about: the kind that is meant to move the soul rather than fill the time. Everything else – the old cities, the grand monuments, the shocking sparsity of the place – simply provides rare exclamation points in the middle of an otherwise long, disturbing paragraph on poverty.

I have completely given up trying to contact Erie by e-mail. I am somewhere in the middle of "Eurasia," as my sixth-grade geography book called it, isolated, lost and in awe of a world that is at least 40 years behind itself.

August 23, 1995

We are someplace in the desert of Kazakhstan. The people are Asian now. Towns are no longer grouped around farmland or industry. They are situated from oasis to oasis. Camel trains connect the two and we have seen them trekking across the bare horizon from one place to another. Everything here is brown. The land is brown. The mud huts – crude approximations of what children make in the sand – are brown. The straw roofs are brown. The grass is brown. It is a god-awful forsaken place. It is surely not land that ever spawned anything human, and it certainly anything human, and it certainly cannot sustain it. Is this the world for which we dream about things like "equality," and "education," and "opportunity," and "a better life"? The whole idea seems preposterous. When you see so much human degradation, you begin to wonder what human really is.

Every time we stop at a station, they run from everywhere to meet the train. They pull old wagons with wooden wheels or wheelbarrows with built-up sides. They come with melons and breads, with apples and oranges. They come poor and trapped – and smiling – to sell. Far too many of them come with far too many melons for this train ever to consume, and most of them drop their arms and their smiles and go home, worse for the wear.

The train churns through it all, however, with some inexorable determination to make it all seem normal. We have become a little world unto ourselves. Classes are regular, workshops on alternative economics and feminist definitions of development are packed, exercise classes and music sessions go on day after day after day. Last night Tabaya, the Sudanese, had a Henna Party. She heard a day or two ago that her parents had finalized her marriage agreement, and last night's ceremony was the traditional way to celebrate the signing of the contract. The singing and body painting and dancing and symbolic offerings of salt and sugar and chocolate and eggs didn't

end until 4:15 in the morning. The train looks a little peaked today
as a result, but at least we all know now that salt symbolizes
excitement in life, sugar, its sweetness and eggs, the raising of a
family. The meaning of the chocolate got lost somewhere between
midnight and dawn. I wouldn't know how. I wasn't there. I heard
about it this morning. I never have been much good at midnight
masses, all-night vigils, third-shift jobs, or parties that last past my
bedtime. Which is early. But I watched her with great interest this
morning. I wondered how she felt going through a time-honored
tribal ceremony with people from all over the globe who had
become for her a very different kind of family. And then I smiled to
myself. Tabaya worked with refugees. She knew very well how
much it meant to be accepted, to be respected, to be supported, to
be embraced by those who had no obligation other than the magic
of humanity to embrace you. "Home," Robert Frost wrote once, "is
where when you go there, they have to take you in." Somehow the
train had become a kind of global home for all of us. We were all
African, all Asian, all Caucasian down deep – and we were all
coming to know it in new ways. Maybe this ceremony meant more
to her in some sense than any other she could possibly have
celebrated, even among her own people.

Tomorrow we will reach Alma-Ata. Late, of course, though I
admit to being baffled by the fact that we can still be late for
something when we had two extra days to get here! I will fax the
article I wrote about the Chinese reorganization of the trip, but it
will not carry half the frustration that I feel about the situation.

When the meetings in Alma-Ata are finished, we will begin the
last segment of the journey to Beijing. We will be transferred from
this Russian train to a Chinese train. The train ride across China will
take almost four straight days and we have heard some wild things
about the design of Chinese trains. The rumors cover a variety of
categories, among them the possibility that the food is served cold;
that the toilets are holes in the floor; and that there is no air-conditioning. And we will be in the Gobi Desert!

I would love to say that I am looking forward to the trip, but I
am not. It's hard to believe that things can get much more demanding than they are right now, but all indicators are that they will. One
thing for sure, the diet will change. There are few replenishment
centers out here in this most Western part of the old Soviet Union.
In fact, there is very little infrastructure of any kind in this part of
the world. People eat a local diet almost exclusively because they

have very few refrigerator cars to transport fresh vegetables across great distances. Just because they grow tomatoes in Azerbaijan doesn't mean that they will have tomatoes in Moscow. We are clearly being fed what the crew was able to bring a long distance without fear of spoilage. So, we have had noodles and three small pieces of meat in gravy for three days in a row now. But I still don't know how I feel about the thought of a menu change. After all, I like noodles.

August 26, 1995

Today would have been my mother and father's wedding anniversary. It is strange to look at my life in comparison to theirs. In the contrast of those lives lies a microcosm of the whole changing world, for people in general, for women in particular, for faith and belief, for state and church. And frankly, whatever the struggles of these years, I prefer my life mightily to theirs. Certainty can be such a stultifying gift in a world in need of questions. They lived the certainties which eventually did not work; we are living the questions for which answers, at least now, are in contest. I'll take the contests anytime. When all the questions of life have been answered, life is over, whether we know it or not.

The program in Alma-Ata was a good one from the point of view of intellectual insight. It was a good cultural experience for most of the train, as well, but not for me. Or maybe, come to think about it, I had a truer cultural experience than any of them.

I went to the hotel business center the minute we arrived in Alma-Ata to fax my last article to Erie. It all seemed so simple: I was first in line and the office was quiet. Good. I knew that it was early morning in the USA, so there shouldn't be any trouble getting the line. Easy. The fee was $6.00 a minute. No problem. I estimated a $25.00 bill. What I did not account for was the fact that the machine was not automatic. They calculated the time with their own hand-held stopwatch. More than that, they calculated from the moment they inserted the paper into the machine. Whether the machine took it or not. Whether they got the line then or not. Whether the document went through or not. As a result, the cost of sending four of the six pages was $90.00. I was in a state of shock. I abandoned the last two pages of the fax – the part that was personal letter – and left the "business center," consoling myself that at least my article was safely arrived in the US and that I'd met another deadline.

The plenary session with the Kazakhi women was an eye-opener. Out here on the far Western border of the old Soviet Union, less than 200 miles from China and strongly Asian in population, they were talking about something called "communitarian feminism," and by that they meant a feminism that "was not radical and not lesbian." The message was clear: They would have no such things here where feminism was going to proceed with reason and peace.

These people, the president of the local women's organization inferred, were going to be "nice feminists," ladylike and loving. "Family," she told us, is "the major value here." She didn't explain herself more, but you knew what she meant from the emphasis she put on every word. These women had no intention of causing the kind of trouble with their feminism which, she implied, women in the West had done. By that she meant, of course, that they would have a feminism where a woman would go on carrying the burden for seeing that everybody else in the family had a good life at the expense of her own. I raised my eyebrows and remembered when I had thought those same things. Then, as the years went by, I saw more and more deeply into the problem and knew that womanhood as womanhood was a more important concept than political "equality," with its very superficial satisfaction with legal niceties. I came to understand that nothing would really change for women until there was indeed a "radical" redesign of ideas and attitudes as well as structures. And the more I said so, the less people found me "nice."

I will watch this place with interest as the years go by. They are a long way from the core of the issue. Yet, they use all the right language and care about all the right things – legislation, education, economics, domestic abuse. They just don't know yet that legislation will not cure the problem. No, the problem is much deeper than the application of cosmetic legislation to a system built on the essential inferiority of women.

At night we had appetizers in the Yurt tent in the courtyard, but we weren't Yurts, and sitting on the ground around a low table under a thick, windowless dome of wool, colorful as it was, did not do the trick. We picked up our plates and went out into the courtyard, where we gave up the romantic thought of a nomad's meal and ate $1.00 plates of Kazakhi *sheslik* (shish-kabobs) and bread instead. Ruth and Gail and Mim and I turned into a crowd in no time. By this part of the trip, the Peace Train has become a nation unto itself. We travel in hordes. Pretty soon you couldn't see who was across the table from you for the stack of empty plates between you. Waiters ran back and forth and up and down the yard trying to figure out bills that defied transcription. It was our first night out in a truly desert climate, with no place to go and nothing to do and no way to know what was coming. We were like kids at the first watermelon picnic of the year.

At about 10:30 p.m., I remembered seeing a sign announcing international telephone booths and fax machines in the post office next door. So, with great abandon and a longing for home, I decided to throw caution, and my wallet, to the wind and send the two pages of personal letter that had been part of the original fax I had taken to the hotel business center in the morning but not sent. The whole process was finished in about 10 minutes. The bill was $6.00. Now I was in shock again! Being a foreigner, whatever your status where you come from, is not an easy thing. Or to put it in the vernacular: being an immigrant turns a professional into a dimwit overnight. I was absolutely unable to function in this society. And I was paying for it, in hard cold cash, as all immigrants do.

As I paid the hotel fax bill, I told them about the difference in prices between their "business center" and the post office. "This is patently dishonest," I said. "Who's getting the extra money?" To her eternal credit, the clerk lowered her eyes as the color rose above the collar of her very swank blouse. "The hotel gets the money," she said. "We" – pointing to the technician with the killer stopwatch – "get none of it." "Well, it is unfair," I continued. "How can they possibly justify this?" "I know it is expensive," the young woman said. And paused. And hemmed a bit. "They tell us to charge foreigners more." They have learned capitalism quickly and well, I thought. And who am I, an American, to complain about it? Greed and exploitation, after all, is our best international trick. In fact, they may have learned it from us. Nevertheless, whatever small consolation it may be, there is more than enough greed to go around in this world, and it is not all white and Western.

The hotel room glowed standard tacky – pressed wood, garish colors, bare floors, no chairs – but, unlike the places we'd been in before, we had warm water and a Western toilet – as opposed to the Turkish ones with their two footrests over a hole in the floor – and a tiny little cradle of a bed with a soft mattress and an open balcony door which, in the evening, turned the sweaty day into cool rain, in the desert, at the foot of black mountains.

The next morning we went to the workshop on "Women and Law" in the grade school that houses "The School of Higher Law of Kazakhstan." I loved the building. It reminded me of the standard brand Catholic schools that I'd studied in myself and in which I had later taught another generation to stretch beyond themselves. These people are clearly stretching for something beyond themselves, as well. Women talked about the place of women in the new constitution of the Republic, their attempts to change the educational system to accommodate the needs of girls and the lack of legal mechanisms to protect them. It was a return to the '70s for most of us, but a poignant one. They are trying so hard to keep the old and make it new. They have no idea that to make anything new you must be prepared to leave the old entirely. It is a trapeze act fraught with danger.

In the afternoon, there was a style show and a concert, both of which I wanted to see but, given the fact that so many others from our wagon seemed to be intent on going to the bazaar and the art museum, I adjusted my plans and prepared for an afternoon of pushing and shoving in an oriental market. I had been lost in Middle-Eastern bazaars, scared out of my wits in dark places and tailed by clerks intent on selling me what I did not want to buy more times than I liked to remember. Everyone should have the experience once. No one, I figured, should have the experience twice. But I was about to.

As I write this, a horse-driven hay wagon is making its way across the vast open seashore to a herd of cattle in the distance. It says a great deal about what is going on here. Two worlds – this transcontinental train and that wobbly hay-wagon – are passing one another, one as different from the other as the face of the earth from the face of the moon. The city of Alma-Ata was a different world from the one I'm used to as well, no matter how similar it looked in some ways.

Standing on the street corner, hailing taxis on a busy street, you could get the idea that this place functioned like all the cities you know – if not Chicago, New York and San Francisco, at least like St. Paul, Harrisburg or Pensacola. Forget it. I glanced quickly at the faxes I'd just received, intent on reserving them for better reading once I was safely back on the train, when all of a sudden there it was. Last sheet, last line of Maureen's letter: "We did not receive your entire article. . . ." I yelped. Ninety dollars to send it and they had not received it. I was down the street on the way to the post office before the taxi ever got the clump of women waiting on the corner. I had five hours to find my article and meet a deadline before the train pulled out into the desert for days. No market, no style show, no concert for me. I never even said goodbye. The hay wagon was racing the train – and the hay wagon was winning.

Alma-Ata

"For my own part," Lord Chesterfield wrote, "I would rather be in company with a dead person than with an absent (read: disinterested) one; for if the dead person gives me no pleasure, at least they show me no contempt; whereas the absent, silently indeed but very plainly, tell me that they do not think me worth their attention." The truth of the statement goes without saying, but now that I have seen it operate, I know more surely how damaging disinterest really is, how it makes a person invisible, and how it renders the invisible a non-person, however competent they might be.

Contracts, visas, and Chinese agreements in hand, the Peace Train with its 230 participants plunged on toward the Chinese border on schedule, despite the refusal of Chinese officials to honor past arrangements to admit the train on August 24 and to allow meetings between Peace Train participants and Chinese women on the Western fringe of the country. All of those arrangements were now in question with Chinese authorities – not to worry. Simple communication problems were surely at the base of the whole misunderstanding, were now being negotiated and would be easily resolved. First things first. First, Alma-Ata. Then,

the Chinese and their clearly groundless concerns.

Alma-Ata, Kazakhstan is a place where street-sweepers still sweep streets and *sheslik* – lamb kabobs, the local specialty – sell at open-air markets for about $1.25 each. The city is about 200 miles from the border of China. On one side of the mountains, a people is struggling haltingly and sometimes crudely to become democratic. On the other side of the intervening mountain range, Chinese nuclear testing grounds, the Kazakhstanis say, threaten "the genocide of the Kazakhstani people." All in all, the place reeks with a blend of the old and the new, Western activism and Asian soul. It is also a place where the feminist movement is being born. But slowly.

Alice-in-Wonderland would have recognized the conversations. There was a rabbit-hole quality to the presentations, all of them sincere, all of them balanced precariously between contemporary concepts and traditional values.

What I learned from the situation in Kazakhstan is that the invisibility of women is one of the women's movement's archenemies, not simply because women have long been invisible to men but because in such societies, women become invisible to themselves. In such a situation, contraditions abound everywhere — most of all, perhaps, in the women themselves. We heard two different voices speak — both of them in the name of women, each of them a variation of the other.

The first voice was from the head of the local feminist organization. She was bright and intense and sure of her brand of feminism. Western feminists, she said, had made mistakes that the Kazakhstanis did not want to make. They could not have "radical and lesbian feminism," she said. What they want is "communitarian feminism." Pressed to discuss the distinction, she said only that they were not against men, that they were simply against institutions that denied women their full human rights.

Then, apparently without sensing the intertwine of the personal and the political, she went on to point out prevailing stereotypes about women. "If a woman is successful in a career," she said, "then people think that everything is not good in her private life. A woman in politics is rare, in arts she is marginal, in science she is industrious but not creative. A woman in the East is a special phenomenon," she concluded. "She combines European independence and Asian domestication. She is part tiger, part snake," she said proudly. The duplicity implied in the statement, the woman's need to balance power by manipulating and wrangling rather than dealing directly

was, presumably, just fine with her. Their real problem, she determined, was simply that "because of Marxist/Leninist ideology, feminism there had been separated from the world movement."

All in all, what Kazakhstani women envisage are very feminine-looking feminists to whom the state gives the special protection and special attention that have been lost with the passing of the Soviet system. "Women," she ended, "are included in all the duties of the new state, but not in its rights."

Yet when she began to list the other things she had in mind — crisis centers for women, gender-free textbooks, freedom from erotica, the end of the wife, mother, prositute stereotypes, the publication of "serious material about women, their personal growth and spiritual development" — the whole hope of making a change in the status of women without causing discomfort in the lives of men evaporated with the speed of mist in sunlight.

Suddenly the tensions of family traditions and the problems of a free society appeared in living color. Unlike the Soviet system in which "the state was equally indifferent and had no mercy either for man or for woman," the new system is hardest on women. Now, it seemed, women know loss and little gain, some theoretical gains in personal freedom and considerable real loss of economic equality and status and voice.

The next morning, women lawyers demonstrated the contradictions best of all. Surveys conducted by teams of women in the area discovered that though 75% of Kazakhstani women feel discriminated against, almost 2/3 of them believe that the inequality of women is "natural," and something to be taken for granted. Only 1/3 of the women surveyed say that struggling for women's rights is something positive for society. "You see the problem," the women lawyers said. "The desire for stability in the society confounds the goals of feminism and human rights."

Kazakhstani women see the violence against women and blame themselves for it. They see the rejection of women and consider it an individual problem, not a societal one. They recognize the misuse, the underdevelopment, the suppression, the marginalization of women, and want "niceness" as well as equality.

Within the month, Kazahkstan will vote for its new constitution. As it reads now, only a man can be president, citizens with rights are described in the male gender, and representative quotas are no longer required, despite the fact that under the Soviet system 30% of all government positions were given by law to women.

Kazakhstani women may indeed face hard times ahead. They want their rights, but they do not want to confront men to get them, and so far no men are stepping forward to do for them what perhaps women must do for themselves. For that, they will have to recognize their visibility and cease to be invisible, even to themselves. The time will surely come. Ask any feminist who remembers the days when she was sure that all a woman needed to be respected as a whole human being was to be "nice." To find that one hardly ever leads to the other creates a serious juncture in the life of any feminist.

But invisibility, I soon discovered, has public as well as personal ramifications. What happens to women in a society where their voices are not heard, where the value of a woman lies almost solely in making life comfortable for a man, where the needs and ideas and social contributions of women are invisible? The answer got clearer than ever at the Chinese border. The terms of the travel agreement were not kept. The train that was promised did not come. The transfer system that was planned did not happen. Instead, the Russian railroad cars were stopped on an embankment and 230 women, some of them elderly, many of them handicapped, all of them laden-down with heavy luggage were dropped off railroad cars into one another's arms instead of being discharged on the station platform for relocation to the Chinese train. One elderly woman, held in a Japanese concentration camp in the Philippines for five years during World War II, described the situation as worse than the internment process she had been through under wartime conditions. Me, I just wondered aloud if a trainload of Western businessmen would have been treated the way these women were. The women behind me, however, were even more astute. Western businessmen, they said, would never have come by train to begin with. And therein lies the difference.

One thing for sure, however. Until women become visible parts of the human race in all its dimensions, until the Fourth UN Conference on Women becomes effective, women will go on being unceremoniously disregarded wherever they are.

"Life is an end in itself," Oliver Wendell Holmes wrote, "and the only question as to whether it is worth living is whether you have had enough of it." The answer for women, as an invisible class, is "No."

We are going into Beijing now with the voices of women across two continents still ringing in our ears. They are calling for economic justice, freedom from personal violence, human rights, systemic inclusion and visibility. The nagging problem now is a simple one: Will the governments of the world agree to such things for women or does someone else still know better what's good for them?

Chinese Border

We left Alma-Ata at about 9:00 p.m. last night, and we are now on the last leg of the trip to the Chinese border. Who knows what awaits us there? The Chinese have already scratched the stop in Urumchi and, on top of it, tried to extort more money out of us to pay for the express train that is supposed to get us to Beijing in time for the meeting. They, of course, are the reason that we have to have an express train. They have delayed our trip by two days, and not only want us to pay for a different train but they are now talking about charging us more for the food, too. No explanation for that whatsoever. My real fear is that they may not let us into China at all if we don't come up with more money. I have no doubt whatsoever that a bureaucracy that is blind, deaf and dumb to anything but instructions from officials who are protected from the consequences of a popular vote is more than capable of that.

Another haywagon has set out for the next herd on the far horizon. I must remember that haywagon minds and transcontinental minds think differently about what is possible, what is fast, and what is necessary.

We are supposed to be at the Chinese border at about 4:00 p.m., another two hours. In the meantime, it is just one long stretch of sear brown stubble bordering a slate blue lake. The two seem incongruous. There is not a boat in sight, not a fisherperson. Just stubble and intermittent herds of cows and every once in awhile, another haywagon. Think of it: day after day after day, every day of your life, you get up and work for the state and then you die.

August 27, 1995

We are on a Chinese train weaving our way slowly and deliberately through the Gobi Desert. It is miles of moon craters, thousands of feet of black rock, days of sand and gravel interrupted occasionally by a squatting mother and child along the tracks, an

anthill of men carrying rocks to lorry carts atilt on the mountain-
sides, a few camels, herds of sheep. In a way the dryness, the
bleakness of the environment seeps into the state of my soul. In
another way, it is a great adventure into another kind of world,
another kind of mind. The beauty of the adventure is that eventually this long trip through nowhere will end for me and I will get
out of it. The horror is that the Chinese people clinging to the
side of these boulder-pocked mountains cannot.

The bleakness in us is more than symbolic, however, more
serious than the climate. There have been a number of losses in
the last 24 hours, the kind that may take some serious reflection
to understand.

It was our last night on the Russian train and we had a party
of grand – and simple – proportions. Someone had a last bag of
Trail Mix. Someone else had a piece of cheese. One cabin brought
a melon they'd gotten from the local women at the last station.
Others had local wines, one bottle of champagne, a small bottle of
vodka, a few cartons of juice for 20 of us. We gave Tatiana and
Marissa, our Russian stewardesses, small baskets of gifts – a few
cosmetics, some packages of chewing gum, organizational pins
and balloons – and an envelope of American money to supple-
ment their meager wages. They had, after all, been living on that
train with us for almost three weeks, sharing a single bunk between them so that one of them was on duty at all times, and
having their own plans affected by ours. We wanted to say thank
you for the little things: for turning on the electricity when we
needed it, for keeping the samovar hot, for smiling always and at
all hours. For standing on the platform and waving us in night
after night. For being there when we wanted them and incon-
spicuous when we did not. For being on call 24 hours a day. We
like them and they like us. We had all managed to give one
another a great deal of space in a setting where there was no
space at all.

We sang old, old songs and laughed at old jokes and got into
deep and sticky conversations about issues far too important to
discuss at midnight. Ruth wanted to know why we went to church
and if we really believed in God. Ruth is a Unitarian, a good one.
She asks all the right questions and hopes that there is a God
who hears them without needing a church bureaucracy to define
the undefinable for her. All in all, the feeling of comraderie and
comfort spilled into the aisles and danced around the corners of

every couchette. We sang songs from every country represented in the car. Then, Tatiana taught us a Russian song that I will never remember and will also never forget. Midge jumped from cabin to cabin with that open-hearted way of hers that saw all of us with equally receiving eyes. Anne and Mickey were their quiet selves, smiling approval, saying little and enjoying every minute of every conversation without a hint of judgement in their eyes. "Doctor D," the neonatologist, told us in a long Texan drawl that if the human body didn't come in a plastic box 12 inches long, she didn't know what to do with it. Mim read the poem she wrote – "It must be Moldavia Again" – and having crossed into Moldavia, it seemed, every time the train turned a corner, we all got into the chorus with a kind of evil glee. Three weeks of laughter came out at once that night. As the car quieted, hours later, I realized that I never in my life dreamed that I would be sorry to leave a dirty, seedy, tacky Russian train. But I was. And I had a lot more reason to be sorry about it than I realized.

The scene at the Chinese border gave new meaning to the term "Chinese Torture Trick." It also gave new meaning to frustration and anger and indignity. In the final analysis, nothing we were told would happen in the process of transferring from one train to another really did. We were told that we would disembark from the Russian train on one platform and that we would simply walk across the platform to the Chinese train on the other side. Instead, the Russian train was made to stop on a steep embankment far from the station, and every woman – old and young, handicapped or hale, tired and loaded with luggage – found herself forced to make a drop of almost five feet while Chinese soldiers simply stood by, staring at us, taking pictures, and doing nothing. Women lifted one another down, helped one another make the jump, carried heavy backpacks and then reloaded them on the rickety vans that finally drove out to the end of the train to take us to the customs hall.

Then, the Chinese, we discovered, had indeed sent a train but not the train we had ordered. This one was short of cars. After days of negotiation about extra charges for the trip, they had solved the question in Chinese style. Since we had a contract which we insisted on their honoring and for which we had, in fact, already paid the previously established price, they simply sent a smaller train. As a result, we all found ourselves in four-bed compartments, $100 short of the services promised in the package we had bought. It was the kind of thing that makes the Western sense of freedom and justice flush with a kind of holy wrath.

We had arrived at the border at 4:00 p.m. We pulled out on the new train loaded with uniformed soldiers, plainclothesmen and staff at 11:57 p.m., tired, hungry, dislocated and sealed off from the outside world. But not without a feeling of barely suppressed triumph. In the first place, we were, after all, on the train. And in the second place, on her way out of a customs hall that was overcrowded, disorganized and frenetic, Gail had passed by an open box of odds and ends sitting unattended in the middle of the floor. And there it was: the old red sweater that she had left at the end of the congo line in St. Petersburg. If ever we needed a good omen, it was now. The look of satisfaction on her face approached the giddy. "You never know your luck in a big city," she said, and all the leprechauns in Ireland were laughing with her. Me included.

China

The nice thing about rumor is that it is always interesting and usually unfounded. The ones about Chinese trains were no different. The train itself was spotless, smooth-running, carpeted and marked by embroidered sheets and pillowcases – much more elegant, in fact, than the Russian train had been. The food was excellent. The staff, the soldiers, the stewardesses were formally and impeccably dressed. "I'll tell you this much," Dorothy said under her breath as staff and soldiers trooped stiffly by, "I'd give anything to have the white-glove concession in this place." But no one smiled at us. It was a lovely but a sterile place. You could feel in your bones the distance between them and us. We had been passengers on the Russian train. I had the eerie feeling that we were inmates on this one, and I could not for the life of me figure out why. One thing for sure: All these people had a job far beyond tending this train. All these soldiers were defending the People's Republic of China from something. But from what?

The train moved out of the station into the desert night, the cars went dark, I stayed awake until far into the morning, propped against the wall in the upper bunk, writing furiously in the glow of the computer screen to get all the details down before my batteries died. I had no assurance whatsoever that I would ever get to charge them again on this train. Every time that evening that I had plugged the transformer into the dead plug and pointed from it to my computer, the stewardess simply waved her white-gloved finger at me, shook her head firmly no and walked away. Their psychologists must be very happy with them: these people are definitely not pleasers.

It was breakfast time before we got the news, and it was more a whisper than an announcement. Then, and only then, did we discover that one of the women, Jill, had been left behind at the border the night before. Her Chinese visa had expired on August 20, and she was not permitted to board the train. Told at another point that she had 10 days' grace, she did not know that the 10 days' extension applied only if she had entered China before the expiration date. So, they boarded all of us first, locked

the train and kept her behind alone. Some of the organizers, realizing the situation at the last minute, had tried to stay with her,
but the Chinese would not permit that and she herself, under the
pressure of time, had waved people off as well.

Hours passed before the word sifted through the train. The
heaviness, the sense of guilt seeped into every conversation. Organizers and delegates both struggled with the dilemma. Why had
we left her alone in the midst of them? How would we find out
what had happened to her? How had it all happened to us so
quickly and without our realizing that it even was going on? And
what would we do the next time some woman was plucked from
our midst, whatever the reason, separated from the group, left to
find her way through an impenetrable system alone? We explained
the situation over and over again to ourselves. We agonized over
it, in fact.

The losses began to dawn on us: We had lost Jill, lost the
warmth of the Russian train, lost our freedom – and even lost our
little bit of air-conditioning apparently. A single, roaring, rotating
fan cooled the hot little cabin as the train raced the raging sun
through a waterless waste called the Taklimakan Shako Desert.
The word means, they tell me, "You Can Go In But You Can't
Come Out." The thought of it is all too real. To be caught here is
to have your soul in captivity forever. To be caught here is to
have your eyes opened in ways you can never ignore again.

The scenery is soul-stretching. The environment is awesome.
The culture is revered. The only problem is that the system is as
barren as the desert. After days of "negotiating" the visas, the date
and time of the border crossing, the right to make the planned
visit to Urumchi, the kind of train we would be on, even the cost
of the meals, the Chinese mode of operation with us is clear now:
They talk and smile and bow and then, at the last minute, when it
is far too late to do a thing about it, they do exactly what they
intended to do all along.

August 28, 1995

Yesterday was a series of small victories – and one large loss.

The victories were minor but important: The first one happened by accident. It was our second night on the train. The
transfer had not been easy and the environment had everybody
on edge. Soldiers were everywhere. They walked the corridors

and watched us as we walked them, too. They made regular inspections of the train. They did not permit our spokespeople to use the public address system to make announcements for us. Instead, they insisted on the announcements being written out for them to give in a sing-song Chinese-English that was not only offensive to our own sense of freedom but was also hard to understand. Point: people were, if not "on edge," definitely wary. I remembered hearing a joke once that seemed to describe the situation best for me. "How do porcupines make love?" the biology teacher asked the students. "Very carefully," a student answered. I was on a train full of porcupines, of peace people, who did not want to make war with anybody, and Chinese military who, for that reason, considered us the enemy. You had to appreciate the irony of it to enjoy it.

At any rate the soldiers were everywhere. Always. Then, on the second morning, I stumbled out of my couchette at dawn, on my way to the washroom, and walked out the cabin door right into the belt-buckle of the tallest Chinese soldier I had ever seen in my life. I was startled. I was also embarrassed. "What in the devil are you doing here!" I demanded in a voice that was a definite throwback to my high school teaching days. "This is a women's sleeping car." I pointed down the corridor. "Get out of here and get out of here right now!" And he left. I was never sure that he understood English, but he definitely understood the message. We never saw him again the entire trip. Victory number one.

Victory number two was a simpler one. I finally wheedled the train people into turning on the electricity for the wall plugs in the corridor. That meant that my computer batteries could now be charged. I had worked on the Alma-Ata article until almost 3:00 a.m. the night before, and I did not have a single battery left. I know that there are still things in the world like pencils and paper but I am, after 12 years of computer work, almost incapable of using them. There was a time in life when I thought nothing of writing my dissertation on a yellow pad with a ballpoint pen, but I certainly cannot write anything of substance or length like that again. I'm not sure if that's a lack of simplicity or a just a lack of penmanship.

The third victory lay in being able to get the air-conditioning turned on in our car once I discovered that other parts of the train already had it.

Everything, in fact, looked very livable again indeed – Chinese communists or no Chinese communists – until one woman in the car decided that none of us could have air-conditioning because she might get bronchitis. I never fail to marvel at the number of "peace people" who resolve group questions unilaterally instead of attempting to find win-win solutions – like swapping beds with someone who doesn't mind the air or simply turning the thermostat up rather than off. Maybe that's why we all find our way to such things as peace movements: not because we're good at making peace but because we need to learn how to control the tendency to war within ourselves. Maybe we should all start giving more credit to the dictators and military men of the world for all the atrocities of the world that they do not commit instead of concentrating exclusively on the ones they do. After all, what proof do we have that if we were in their place that we would do better? I mean, anyone who can arbitrarily deprive people of air-conditioning in the Gobi Desert ought to understand how easy it is to start a war. And if she doesn't, I do. I hate heat.

The next problem made me forget the heat in a hurry. We used to have a Sister in the community whose favorite saying was, "Watch how you word your prayers. You may get what you want." I don't remember if I prayed to get out of the heat on that couchette ceiling or not, but just to be on the safe side, I never will again. Being in a double-decker cabin made age and infirmity relative. I had wound up in a top bunk. The second night I fell trying to climb down – which, tell the Chinese, is why I never registered for a four-bunk cabin in the first place. After a hot and miserable night spent testing every joint in my body and waiting for dawn, the count is one bruised left side, one broken toe, and one middle finger either sprained or smashed. I have been in the "hospital car" all day, getting the sleep I lost last night, taking pain pills and wondering how a writer types with a splinted hand. Well, I'll tell you: one letter at a time.

All day long I have sat at the train window and watched rural China go by: the Gobi Desert, Shanxi province, mile after mile of adobe villages, bare brown mountains, hand-hewn human cave dwellings carved out of the side of the hills – home to 10% of the population of this province, the guidebook says – and, as far as the eye can see, the mind can imagine and the soul can stretch, tier upon tier of perfectly symmetrical gardens blooming out of dry, cracked earth. The Yellow River has gone racing by, thin and wasted, leaving the barren land to peasants already over-taxed. China is a monstrous place, full of quiet beauty, full of obscene hardship.

Mount Everest is in China. And so, too, are almost one-fourth of the population of the entire globe, 25% of the human race. In one country. In a land mass smaller than Russia, smaller than Canada. That's 319 people per square mile, as opposed to 73 people per square mile in the United States. Sixty percent of them are in agriculture and fishing. Eighty percent of them are able to write their names, but who knows how much more. It is a nation of beauty, a nation of barrenness.

Outside the train was a bucolic scene of everything romantically rural. Inside the train, soldiers and plainclothes police walked the corridor protecting the People's Republic of China, it had finally become clear, from 230 old women. "No, not from old women," Teresa Wilson, one of the organizers of the Peace Train project and a woman of wisdom and purpose, later corrected me. "From new ideas." Yes. At every station, the local Chinese populace were swept off the platforms first before the women were permitted outside the train for ten minutes of exercise in the open air. Like Lenin being transported through Germany, we were being taken across China in a sealed train, a virus to be kept from people who might be tempted to succumb to the very ideas of peace, freedom and development that had infected us.

Beijing

The last day on the train was a long, slow one. We packed and repacked and fussed and played end-games all day long: "Here's my card. . . . I'll send you that . . . Listen, we'll have lunch at the conference. . . . Please call when you get to New York." All the things you say to people with whom you have just shared a life-changing experience but will never see again, sincere as you are, grateful as you can be.

Beijing stretched along the railroad tracks like a long, quiet dragon. High rise buildings dotted the skyline, rooftop signs blinked on and off with the feverish energy of New York City. Broad sweeping highway systems stretched for miles on each side of the train. I wrinkled my brow a bit. This did not seem to be the city I was led to expect. Where were the shanty towns? Where were the masses of poor huddled along the tracks? Where were the swarms of people queued and tight, sweaty and moving in great, silent herds down tiny, sinuous alleys? Then, over the public address system of the train came the strains of "Auld Lang Syne" – in Chinese. It was a strange moment. Lined up along the corridor windows, waving at passing trains full of astonished Asians and suddenly very, very awake after three long weeks on the road, the women of the Peace Train laughed and cried – and sang – at the same time. We were coming into Beijing 12 hours later than planned, deprived of our plans, cramped in our quarters but we were here despite it all. We had survived. We had prevailed. The Chinese had won all the battles but not the psychological war. In the end, it was the pacifists who had pursued and persisted and prevailed.

The train station, clean and empty, awaited us like a yawning mausoleum. No bustle here. No throngs of people. No come and go, push and shove, run and hustle of Kennedy station at noon. No, like every other station along the Chinese line between Alma-Ata and Beijing, the platform had been emptied of people. There was only our one train, the alighting delegation, a few greeters and a longer caravan of buses than I had ever seen in my life.

In the cabin, I took one last-minute stock of luggage – the backpack, the stewardess case, the computer – and that's when it happened. Clothes I can do without; books and papers are replaceable; souvenirs are meaningless to me. The one thing I cannot do without, the one thing I am compulsive about is my computer. If something happens to it, the worst happens to me. Everything is gone: my journal, my articles, my research data. So, I checked one more time, "for good measure," to make sure that the computer and all its peripherals were safe and securely packed in its very small and very compact case. To offset the effects of jet lag, I store everything in the same place at all times. Except that this time they weren't where they should have been. Things had been moved. The batteries had been taken from one set of pockets and put in another. The transformer cord, always neatly wrapped around the unit and secured by rubber band, was loosened. The papers in the side of the case were in disarray. Someone had been in my computer. Welcome to Communist China where journalists are suspect, political criticism is forbidden and social analysis is the province of the state. I stood there shaken for a moment. And then I saw the next thing. There, on the end of the wagon table was the smallest pocket camera I had ever seen. The person who had gone through my computer case had left a tiny camera behind in the process. I smiled a little and put the camera in my purse. This could be one of the most interesting rolls of film I would ever have developed.

Young men in Hewlett-Packard T-shirts marked "volunteer" met every railroad car separately, carrying roses, smiling on cue. A contingent of local women bustled along the cars, smiles on their faces, shaking hands and distributing flowers for the benefit of a small video crew that tagged obediently along behind the official Chinese hostesses, spotlights blazing. The welcome was very fine, very formal but there was something missing. What's wrong with this picture, I kept asking myself. What's wrong with this picture?

Outside the station, people lined the route, held back by the police, cleared far away from the buses. A police escort led us down an empty highway in one of the largest cities in the world. I couldn't get it out of my mind: What's wrong with this picture?

We were taken directly to a conference registration center to be processed like immigrants on Ellis Island. "Papers, please.

Number, please. Passport, please. Picture, please. Money, please," and it was all over. We had been counted and labeled and carted to hotels in the space of an hour. They are an efficient people, these Chinese. When they decide they want to do something, there is no doubt whatsoever that they can do it. After all, with a population of 1.2 billion people, what is another 40,000 or so to them?

It was only outside in the parking lot of the registration center that I began to realize what was missing. The parking lot was empty. There were no people around at all. No friends, no visitors, no international WILPF officers, no onlookers – no journalists. And, God knows, journalists are everywhere. Journalists had swarmed around us in every country we'd visited. This was, after all, no ordinary train. But there were no journalists milling around here waiting to ask exhausted women how 25 days of life on the line had been for them. Then, suddenly, one woman ran into the center of the group from behind a bus parked on the far side of the square. "No one, absolutely no one," she said, "has been allowed to come to the train to meet you." The Chinese do everything by allotted tickets, but there were no tickets issued for the train station. Only people assigned to the task of greeting us were allowed into the area. Clearly, the Chinese did not want the delegates of 230 Non-Governmental Organizations loose in front of cameras and microphones. We were in the city but we were not free – and neither was anyone else. "This pass," the Italian journalist who had managed to slip into the area unseen hissed, fingering her press card, "is worth nothing. Nothing." I cringed a little inside. I was there under press credentials. I was the enemy, too. I had come to write about women, not about the Chinese, but how you could not write about the Chinese government? They had, after all, managed to make themselves the story.

It was almost 4:00 a.m. before we got to bed. Here we were in a hotel room, unpacked and totally drunk with the prospect of days of hot water, soap and a bathroom that was clean, stocked and operable. How can anyone be expected to sleep at such an exciting time as that?

The NGO Forum

The next day, Wednesday, August 30, we spent navigating around Beijing to pick up press credentials and try to find a pass for an opening event that no one had told us required a pass. The Olympic Stadium, built to house the Olympics which, in the end, the Chinese never got to host, holds 20,000 people. There are 38,000 people registered for the NGO/UN Conference. Go figure.

We began the registration process at the Beijing International Conference Center at 1:00 p.m. The "Center" is blocks long, one building after another, some of them hotels, some of them sports arenas, some of them auditoriums and some of them meeting sites. Nothing is really "centered" anywhere. You go here for this and there for that. After weeks on a train, I was about to spend weeks in an international infantry corps. And nobody told me any of this when I joined.

Hours later, we literally stumbled onto an unmarked convention kiosk where, surprise, they were giving away tickets to the Opening Ceremony. We walked into the stadium across the street from the convention center at 4:00 p.m. In over six hours, all we had managed to do was to get one pass and one ticket. That is, it seems, about the amount of time it takes to get anything done in Beijing. Well, the wag says, "If you want things to be 'just like home,' stay home." Good advice.

The opening event was a *tour de force* of Chinese organization, creativity, scope and sheer weight of numbers. At one point in the show, we estimated that there were at least 3500 performers on the field at once. Some say more than that. "Uncle," Gail croaked beside me when the field filled up and filled up and filled up with thousands of costumed Chinese and would not stop filling. I agreed. No wonder the 14 countries who border China, and all the rest of Eurasia with them, spend so much time worrying about these people and the security of their national boundaries. If the Chinese, pressed for resources and drained by overpopulation, ever decide to get up and walk out of this country looking for space in someone else's country, they might well outlast the resistance of the rest of the world on the basis of numbers alone.

At the same time, the event was a milestone in my own experience of womanhood. No Olympic Games could possibly capture the spirit that permeated this massive outpouring of womanhood. I had been in military extravaganzas, in football playoffs, in some of the largest church ceremonies in the world. In all of them, in most of life, I and others like me were the minority, the other, the onlookers at events that really belonged to men, that were directed by men and staffed by men and performed by men. Here, the stands were full of women, thousands and thousands of women. The performers, by and large, were women, the symphony orchestra of Beijing that filled the arena with bright and brilliant music from every continent on earth was a women's orchestra with a woman conductor, the speakers were all women, the roars of the crowd were women's roars. This was my world and it was a real one. It had been too long invisible but it was real nevertheless.

The sheer improbability of it all caught me completely off guard. I saw with my own eyes what concerns men about the women's movement: the fact of the matter is that these women really could run the world. And, for the first time in my public life, I was in a public gathering that extolled a woman's full capacity – not simply her "virtues," not only her motherhood, not primarily her servanthood or, worse, not essentially her "uniqueness" as the "first woman who," or "the only woman who," or the "token woman who" broke solitarily into the ranks of manhood. This was about all women and all of a woman's abilities – intellectual, physical, artistic. I thought at one stage of this program that never seemed to end that I would simply stop breathing from the sheer immensity of it all. We were not exceptions. We were half the human race.

On the other hand, the stadium was also dotted with men, plainclothes security men we were all now sure, keeping sentry over the dangers of untamed ideas. One thousand of them against 20,000 of us, all physically bigger, all watching, all armed. That's how men balance out equality with women – by force, by power, by threat. They keep the money, and the offices, and the uniforms, and the collars, and the guns and tell us that God wants it this way. Yeah, sure.

It makes you wonder what they're afraid will happen to them if women ever do end up in charge of anything significant. Certainly it couldn't possibly be worse than what is happening to the world without us.

After the program, we walked through a sea of buses to ride with Peace Train people back to their hotel for a group farewell party that did not, in the end, materialize. We walked from lobby to ballroom to mezzanine and found little clumps of people waiting in each place, but no one had seen any real evidence of a party. Teresa and Jack Wilson, people I had really come to like on the train, suggested that we make our own party. Without Teresa, who invited me on this little odyssey, I would never have been on the Peace Train in the first place. Without Jack, I .wouldn't have laughed nearly so much. So, we went downstairs to "the island" – a hunk of cement in the middle of a pool of recycled water – and drank warm Chinese beer. I smiled to myself. In my country we import paper lanterns and goldfish to authenticate our Chinese restaurants. Here in Beijing, the Chinese restaurant was going to great pains to look Western. Alice in Wonderland made the point years ago: sometimes up is down and down is up. The four of us solved the great problems of life and took a cab back down the long, wide, darkened avenue to the Minzu Hotel in the center of Beijing, where the Chinese could keep their eye on the foreign press with comfort and ease.

August 31, 1995

We slept in this morning, not because I wanted to but because my body betrayed me. Two alarm clocks never penetrated the bliss that came with being in a bed that wasn't moving as I slept, one that allowed me to roll over in one fell unconscious swoop without having to ease myself around from point to point to avoid falling out of a moving bed. I loved being on that train, but I loved being off of it, too.

Huairou, the site of the NGO Forum, is about 60 km outside of Beijing. It takes a one hour and 45 minute cab ride to get there from the other side of Tiananmen Square. And one hour and 45 minutes to get back at night. Four hours a day just to get to the meeting site and back. "Oh, this is great," I thought. "I might as well be commuting from Morristown, New Jersey to Manhattan, New York." True, the buses run every 20 minutes, just as the

Chinese said they would. The Chinese did not say two other things, however: The first thing they failed to tell us is that the buses run from the hotel for only one hour every morning in 20-minute intervals. The first bus goes at 7:00 a.m. The last bus goes at 8:00 a.m. If you miss that one, you are over 60 kilometers – about 40 miles away from the meeting, with no way to get there but cab. The second thing they never told us is that at the end of the day, the buses run only from Huairou, the NGO Forum site, to the Worker's Stadium on the outskirts of the city. From there you are simply left to get a cab to wherever they have put you in Beijing.

A city of over 10 million people, where everywhere is a long way from anywhere. I think I am beginning to understand the principle behind the game of Chinese Checkers.

The delegates who live in Huairou have it every bit as hard, if not harder, than we do. At least cabs and buses take us door to door – whatever the time element, whatever the cost. The hotels bring us hot water at night for tea, deliver the daily paper to the door, serve hot food, have money changers and air-conditioning. People living in Huairou walk for blocks to a conference site that is itself an area of 140 acres filled with over 50 tents and at least 20 buildings, none of which are numbered consecutively. They live in walk-up apartments, cooled only by fans, and walk the streets for the rest of their needs.

The question, of course, is why a city that wanted to host an international conference is seemingly so intent on making it difficult to have one. The answer may be getting clearer by the day. I figure this way: In China, I have discovered, no group is permitted to function unless it is certified, monitored and censored by the government. In China, therefore, every organization is a government organization – including the non-governmental ones. Any group here that is not approved by the government, not working under the aegis of the government, constitutes a dissenting group. And these people do not deal gently with dissenters. To the mind of the Chinese communist, dissent is not simply another way of thinking; dissent is revolution. The daily newspaper here is a paean of self-congratulation. It tells only good news. And whatever the government does is good news.

To us, on the other hand, the value of a non-governmental organization lies precisely in the fact that it brings to government another way of thinking that comes from identification with the people and immersion in the non-governmental dimensions of society, where the needs of the people, rather than the agendas and operations of the federal government dominate.

With those very different categories in mind, the picture in my mind begins to clear considerably. To the Chinese, NGO delegations are all troublemakers by definition. And they want those types as far away from the UN Conference, the official one, as they can get them so they can't stir up trouble. We call it "lobbying," a time-honored democratic practice aimed at influencing elected officials. They call it trouble.

The strategy of separating the NGO Forum from the UN Conference, then, is a very deft one. By separating the two sites by miles and restricting easy access, the NGO delegates can have their carnival if they so choose. In Beijing, however, the real work will be done by governmental delegations. That's what they think. We'll see.

Huairou is not a "conference center." Huairou is a city. Conference sites are spread throughout the town, up hills and down, from one end of the area to the other. We plodded through booths marked B10-12, 29-37, past the Peace Tent, through the Asian tent, over to the Tibetan tent, beyond France and Europe, Africa and Islam. Whatever happened to the numbers in-between may remain an eternal mystery. We never did find Tent 17, the one I walked miles looking for. Instead, we ate fast-food Chinese noodles on the street with women from Kenya, Chicago, California, the Philippines and Ireland. Forget the logistical problems. The whole effort is worth it. In what other situation can this happen?

The streets teemed with women from every part of the world. African queens swept by in bright colors and turbans, Asian women in silk wrap-arounds, Muslim women in *chadors,* Westerners in shorts and slacks. These were the women who were going to agree on a Platform of Action for all the women of the world? I'll believe it when I see it.

I went to the NGO orientation meeting and learned more about the process of turning a jamboree into a political presence than anyone needs to know. The women giving it were impressive professionals who knew the system and were more than adept at functioning in it. I sat in the auditorium and wondered how many people realized that underneath the old regime, burrowing its way to the center of the system, the women's movement was seeding a whole new world.

I went to a workshop called "The Status of Women's Study Programs Around the World," and marveled that Fiji and Canada were grappling with the same problems: a cooled revolution and domesticated rebels. Dr. Rita Hoffman Imarov, Professor of Women's Studies at the University of Ottawa, had the kind of fire in her voice that fueled this movement and makes it real yet. At least for some of us. At least for those who first saw the Promised Land. Whether younger women know yet that they still have things to do for themselves that we cannot do for them any longer, I am not so sure. One thing I do know, however. When this crowd of younger women, educated, employed, raised in tele-vision-land with its plastic expectations and happy endings, dis-covers that though all the institution doors look open, all the doors are glass and all the ceilings are low – that they may now be allowed in places their mothers never were, but they will not be able to progress there to the same degree or at the same pace as their male colleagues – we will have the best prepared group of feminists in the history of the world. Then, the boycotts will come; then the strikes will come; then the lawsuits will come; then the demonstrations will come. Then look out.

The program for the day listed 28 pages of optional work-shops, lectures, film programs and panels, over 5000 of them for the week. I learned as much from the titles as I did from the lectures. There were women from every part of the globe, every interest under the sky talking to women from every other part of the world, every other interest under the sky. In fact, there may be too many to make any sense out of anything. All I know about this place so far is that it is a zoo without a keeper. It has no center. Very few people know anything about anything, and no one I've met so far knows everything about everything. Thoreau had it right: go to a lake in the middle of the woods and write down whatever you are thinking and that will be enough. Trying to make sense out of the futile has very little appeal to me.

The day had a touch of the surreal about it. How was it that we could have all these people intent on the equality of women and not have it? I began to understand John Lennon's plaintive cry, "I'm not the only one." At the sight of the swarm after swarm of women, floating down the hills, crossing into classrooms and auditoriums, demonstrating on the streets for their sisters – for their daughters – my heart, long-starved for more than principle, rose up with a new kind of hope.

I got a cold toasted cheese sandwich and soggy french fries from room service for supper. Welcome to Beijing, home of the Peking Duck.

September 1, 1995

It was pouring rain in Beijing this morning and got worse as the day went on. Huairou was a swamp by the time we got there, and I was soaked to the bone three times before mid-afternoon. Pretty soon I simply stopped trying to go from building to building and settled down in one site to listen to presentations that I might not have chosen by instinct. It was a great experience. I learned a lot.

Asian women are beginning to organize for social change. There is a growing conviction among women that the religions that sustain them are also, in many cases, the chains that bind them, that what men have declared as religious truth has been defined only by men and to men's advantage.

The girl-child is in danger. Trafficking in young females is on the rise. Children are bought from poor villagers for bonded labor, prostitution, domestic labor and "marriages" that start in abuse and end in abandonment. I felt myself get physically sick at the thought of 10-year-old girls lost and left in cities that prey upon them as if they are rabbits in a barnyard, while the men of the world watch the men of the world pluck the world of whatever pleases them. Now, the sociologist from India said, they are even beginning to find the bodies of young girls dumped outside of villages, eyes gone, hearts taken, kidnapped to harvest the organs that are fast becoming a new black market business. Girls. Girls' bodies only. Why girls? Because their organs are stronger or healthier or more universally matchable? Oh no, nothing so complimentary as that. They are girls' bodies because girls aren't worth anything to begin with in this world.

There were rumors that Chinese security officers intruded on a workshop given by Tibetan sympathizers in an attempt to confiscate their materials. "Aw, come on," I thought. I listened politely, but deep down I knew that there simply had to be some kind of misunderstanding. After all, this is not a James Bond movie. This is a UN Conference. Of women. And it is 1995. Things like that don't happen anymore. Famous last words. Every newspaper in the world carried the story, and I was right here and missed it. So much for on-site reporting when it is pouring rain and you are squashed in the middle of a sea of 40,000 umbrellas.

In a sense it was silly to stay in Huairou in weather like this. The seminar rooms were more packed than ever from people trying to get out of the hard and steady rain. The tent grounds were too muddy to even attempt a walk through the exhibits. Everything about me squished, my shoes, my slacks, even my cloth shoulder bag. But I made up my mind that nothing was going to interfere with what I knew would be one of the highlights of the conference for me. One of the offerings of the day was a one-woman show given by a Scandinavian actress entitled "The Ibsen Women." It was a long time till 5:00 p.m. But it was worth it.

The auditorium was tiny, unequipped and bare. There were no sets because there were no hooks from which to hang them, no flies from which they could suspend. "We can't use our scenery," the actress said, "so we will have to create the scene in your mind alone." And she did. I felt my spirit soar and dash as she performed. This was high art at the barest possible level. This was the obscene exposure of a woman's life – in all its facets, under all its masks. I have gone to concerts in Brussels and symphonies in Rome, but I have never been more moved than I was by these two women, one an actress, the other the flautist whose plaintive music burrowed into my soul and set every scene. The naive woman, the angry woman, the depressed woman, the exploited woman, the woman become female when she wanted to be womanly – they were all there. The discussion after the vignettes tried to understand how 100 years ago a man had been able to understand the plight of women so well. Maybe, I thought, it really is possible after all. Maybe there is more than one Ibsen out there who knows the size of this social sin and will repent it.

I bought medicine balls in a Chinese store, and we left Huairou exhausted and drained but full of a new kind of energy. Ruth and Gail and I shared a cab into Beijing. We are all dispersed now. Ruth was at one hotel, we at another, so it took a little maneuvering but, in the end, we managed to meet for supper in our dining room at the Minzu Hotel. It's a very, very Chinese hotel where few of the staff speak English and where four waiters huddle around every table, snatching plates away, running to get dish after dish, hovering around to pick up dropped napkins and standing behind your chair to pour the last drop from every beer bottle for you. It gives a kind of ethereal color to an otherwise mottled day.

Each night there is a new discovery: pickled cucumbers, Chinese breads, *ciue ciue* sauce and little slices of language hard to say the first time and impossible to remember thereafter. The whole life process here takes total concentration: how to get around, how to eat, how to find out what in god's name is really going on. And every minute of it has been worth the effort. How else do we get out of ourselves, how else do we learn to respect others, except by going out of ourselves and doing things their way?

September 2, 1995

Today, I made up my mind, was going to be better paced. We would stay in town to begin the UN briefings and make it an earlier evening. I called Soon Young Yoon, the UN liaison to the NGO Forum. Soon Young is a Korean-American woman who is bright, personable and very, very competent. She has the capacity to organize the world and make it look like a part-time job. My intention was to check the next day's briefing schedule, but I also mentioned in passing that I had heard a rumor among the journalists in my hotel that the Chinese had stopped the publication of the NGO newspaper, *The Forum,* because of the Tibetan demonstration. Was that true? "I can't tell you anything," she said, "but if I were you I would go to Huairou today to see what happens." Cryptic but clear. We raced to the bus half-awake, walked the streets of Huairou looking for coffee, and went to the morning plenary on "The Rise of Conservatism." The intention was to go from there to the Press Office for a quick backgrounder and then back into the city to prepare for the next day's work at the UN Conference site. The problem is that I followed my instincts instead of my schedule.

"Catholics for a Free Choice," a group of US Catholics who support reproductive rights, had a small room and a big crowd. Women pressing to get in stood craning and cramming in a line that ran almost half the length of the long hallway. Something had to be going on. I slipped around them and headed for the back door of the small room. The room was packed to its edges, but the audience was dead quiet, rapt, totally engaged. Four women were explaining how they could stay Catholic in a church that rejects women and calls the rejection God's will. Women packed the doorways, perched on the windowsills, sat on the floor. Some in hope. Some in disbelief. Clearly, the topic impels. After all, the question "Does God like women or not?" is no small problem for women these days.

But all of a sudden the conversation took a turn away from the theology of the problem to the politics of the problem: Why was the Vatican in the UN Conference to begin with? They are not really members in the full sense of the word, the speaker said. They are a religion, not a national government in the truest sense of the word, she argued. The head of the delegation is an American citizen, not a citizen of the Vatican, she pointed out. They speak from the perspective of a creed, not a constitution, she went on. I began to wonder. On the other hand, if the UN admits them, the UN must think they belong, I thought. But the arguments continued. The Vatican and Switzerland, the speaker explained, are simply non-member states with permanent observer status gained by, some say, a kind of geo-political chicanery years ago. Now they have the power – like Russia, China, the USA, every other nation-state in the UN – to block the proceedings of the rest of the world from the imperious vantage point of less than half a square mile of national territory.

There could be little doubt that the question was a real one. Whether or not anyone would bother to address it in the light of the *real politique* is anybody's guess. After all, there are all kinds of protectorates, governments, alliances and federations in the UN already. There is no single model for membership apparently. And yet, at the same time, this thing makes the bizarre look sensible. As a result, "Catholics for A Free Choice," the organizers of this particular workshop, are circulating a petition to have the Vatican removed from the UN. On the way out the door, women signed it with their jaws set. Conscience can be such a troublesome thing.

I couldn't get the question off my mind: We need value discussions in the public arena, of course, but what is the line between maintaining a personal religious posture and making its development impossible for everybody else? The church itself teaches us to realize that "people of good will" may agree on principles but disagree on the means to attain them. They allow it on the topic of capital punishment and nuclear weapons, for instance. It is only on subjects of women and sexuality where they speak in absolutes, it seems. These are complex times. New science, new physics and new technology are bringing old ideas under new scrutiny again everywhere. Biology is changing our idea of what is "natural." We are learning more and more about the cosmos everyday, and the more we do, the more it puts old theories, old truisms in question. All those things bubble up and spill over at a conference like this where religion is so often the justification for the oppression of half the human race.

By the end of the meeting, Filipino women were finger-pointing and shouting at other women in the room that they couldn't be Catholic unless they "respected our Holy Father" and accepted his decrees. "To be a Catholic," they insisted, a person must "keep the commandments, receive the sacraments and accept the authority of the Pope." But what does that definition say about the theologians who contested the selling of relics and the theology of the theocratic state? What does it say about Bartolomeo de Las Casas, who contested the revocation of the Papal Bull that declared Indians fully human? Did those people cease to be Catholics when they began to think – and to say so? Sticky.

I thought for a moment that the meeting would have to be scuttled. Women were shouting at one another, banging on desks for silence, clearly dividing into camps. Then I saw happen before my very eyes the kind of nonviolent presence in a time of tension which I have so long respected. With tempers at the flare point and patience at a premium, Frances Kissling, portrayed by the ultra-right-wing as a hysterical radical and thought of by others who fear the questions as an incorrigible troublemaker, stepped into the center of the room, called for silence and preached a word of peace. She laid ground rules for the conversation in a respectful voice. She called on people in an even-handed way. She brought thought to fire and she taught a lesson in peacemaking that few in that room will ever forget. In 25 years in the peace movement, I have not seen it done any better than this on such a volatile subject. I thought two things: First, the whole church could profit from a discussion such as this in just this tone and tenor. Second, we must learn to be careful whom we call the "enemy." One of Jesus' parables came to mind. "Behold, an irritating widow," I thought, who knows injustice when she sees it, refuses to forego the question and presses on without flagging for resolution of it, but whose heart is gold and whose presence is soft. Be forewarned: Those kind are formidable foes. Those kind have the capacity to perdure.

The session with "Catholics for A Free Choice" was intense, but the next meeting matched it for interest and challenged it for fervor. "The Islamic Assembly of North America" presented itself in the form of a 30-year-old American Muslim male from Chicago who gave a one-hour lecture on "Islamic Alternatives to the Platform for Action," the discussion of which made the Catholic fight look like a Sunday school picnic. Some Muslim women resented the very fact that a man purported to lecture them about the Koran. Others were upset that he was an American rather than an Arab. One of them refused to speak to him in English; she used Arabic, "the language of the Koran," to let him know that she had more claim on the text than he did. The rest of them contested his right to assume the position of an Arab pope. "No one speaks for Islam," they said. "The Koran speaks for itself."

But they didn't want "cultural imperialism" either, they said, meaning that they didn't want a white Western woman's platform given to them for ratification that neglected their own culture and values. So who knows how they'll go in the end? Will they align themselves with the women of the world who are clamoring for "reproductive rights, equality and resources" or with the "honor" that comes from the Koran for "the wombs that bore us." Whatever the resolution of the question at this meeting, the matter is far from settled, I bet, in Islam. I remember the first ministers, priests and pastors, too, who told women that they couldn't work outside the home, couldn't get theology degrees, couldn't use feminine pronouns in liturgies, couldn't be ordained. That's called going the wrong way on a one-way street.

We looked for hours for a Chinese man by the name of Alex to get me a Sprint membership, but we never did find him. In fact, I haven't been able to find any Chinese whom they say exists. I am beginning to think that it is all a great national scam. If they don't know the answer to something, they simply pass you off to someone else who knows less until you get tired of trying to find out. They're very nice people and they want to be helpful. So, they will spend literally hours with you in an attempt to solve your problems but, at the end of the day, Alex still does not exist. And the sooner you figure that out, the more time you'll have to spend doing something besides look for Alex. It's all right, I don't want a Sprint membership anyway.

September 3, 1995

Just when I think that something can't get any more tangled than it is, it gets worse. I stayed in Beijing today to go to the NGO/UN briefing and never got into it. There is simply no way to find out what is going on or where it is going on or who can get in there if you ever do find out where it is. I have an idea that I am going to cover the UN Conference in front of a TV set or on the street talking to delegates privately. Well, maybe that is the story.

I did luck into the press conference with the Chinese Organizing Committee today, however. I happened to be standing in a hall when they and the cameras went by into the audience hall. Another reporter who had also figured out that something was happening that we should know about simply grabbed me by the elbow and dragged me through the crowd with her. In China, that's called "having connections."

The press conference completely frustrated the Western press. It was like watching a greased eel smile. Reporters did everything they could to find out what changes were going to be made in the wake of the complaints about security excesses, harassment of speakers and the confiscation of workshop materials. The COC simply called the whole thing "a grave misunderstanding" that was "old news," smiled and went on to other topics. But, when pressed over and over again, the message in the final analysis was loud and clear: "Attacks on the national sovereignty of China" – sympathy for Tibet, in other words – will "not be tolerated." Then, after 10 questions, they called off the press conference. It is an interesting situation: a totalitarian state with a smiling face.

One good thing happened, though. The Chinese Organizing Committee assured the press that double the number of tickets for tomorrow's opening ceremony at the Hall of the People had already been sent to press hotels. See? No need at all for all this complaining about not being able to get into things and not being able to cover what we cannot attend. They are practically delivering the tickets to our doors now. I would simply go back to the hotel and pick one up.

Perhaps the greatest challenge of them all here comes out of trying to understand the city of Beijing itself. This is not the Soviet Union where store shelves are bare and cities are dour. This is not Communism Eastern European style. This is a sparkling, beautiful place with a steadily rising standard of living, a flare for beauty and an edge of Western capitalism in a Communist contour.

I had lunch with a couple of journalists. Esther is an ordained minister from Switzerland, whose interest in the women's movement comes from a very rarified perspective, but for whom the language barrier made that difficult to explore in great depth. Pat, on the other hand, specializes in religious coverage for a number of places in the USA. The nice thing about journalists is that they are thinkers, analysts, listeners. It's their business. It was an oasis of calm in the Tower of Babel. Pat is extremely knowledgeable and very nice about it. She talks down to no one, learns from everyone, and teaches a good deal as she goes. She is the kind of woman that makes a woman feel good about being female.

We got back to the hotel early but totally frustrated. In the first place, there are no tickets here. I have just spent 30 more minutes with three more smiling Chinese, who assure me that the tickets are at our embassies. Just go to your embassy, they assure us, and you can get your tickets there. (Lights go off in my head. This sounds to me like a variation on the Chinese-named-Alex story again.) "How many tickets went to each Embassy?" I ask, making a quick calculation of the number of US reporters who are now scrambling to get them. "Oh, many," they say. And smile.

The second frustration arises from the fact that the UN Conference opens in the midst of the ongoing NGO Forum in Huairou. Where is Houdini when you need him? How we divide ourselves between the two – miles apart – and still determine what happened at both is anybody's question. For instance, we have no tickets for tomorrow's opening ceremony, no assurance that we'll get into anything and no sure way to know what is really going on where or how best to divide the day. I think I'll just drop out for a while tonight – no meetings, no interviews, no document review. I need to sit and let the world go by on its own for a change. After all, there's only so much frustration that anyone can endure. Even me.

September 4, 1995

I spent most of yesterday and much of this morning trying to track down tickets for the Opening Ceremony. You guessed it: Not here. Not there either. The US Embassy "had a few" but not many, and the person who has them isn't there anyway. OK, so I'm not

Marco Polo, but one thing I know for sure: He couldn't have had it much harder in China than I have, than the whole international press has it, in fact. I am at this moment sitting in an auditorium waiting to watch on closed-circuit television what is probably being shown on the television in my hotel room. Press passes to the plenary weren't distributed until about 20 minutes ago. We waited in a line that ringed the convention center twice and, in the final analysis, almost no one got passes. Then, the US briefing that was scheduled for 2:00 p.m. was postponed until 5:30. There are no schedules posted anywhere. The trick is simply to camp here from 8:00 a.m. until the end of the day and see if anything happens. At the same time, the word is that Hillary Clinton is speaking at the NGO Forum in Huairou at 9:00 a.m. tomorrow morning. That means that those of us in Beijing will have to be on the road by 6:30 a.m. if we want to be there for it. You get the distinct impression trying to cover this story that you are arm-wrestling with an octopus. A blind octopus. A deaf, dumb and blind octopus. An unfriendly octopus indeed.

Anyway, isn't this fun? Chinese fire drill; Chinese jigsaw puzzle; Chinese torture trick. Synonyms. All synonyms. My advice: read it on Internet. Just kidding. I, too, get sour sometimes.

On the other hand the real story may not be in the convention hall at all. As I sit in this auditorium waiting to watch the opening plenary on closed-circuit television, the rest of the world press is walking into the press auditorium now and they are women, black and brown and yellow, in huge turbans and colorful sashes, in silks and saris, in corn rows and dangling earrings the size of dinner plates. Peoria, take note. White, Western, male hegemony is coming to a pathetic end: feared, fearing, suspected and, sometimes, even deeply, deeply resented.

I stayed in the hotel and wrote an article this morning. The room was cool and quiet and I loved being there alone. I had had all of the thick, sweating, confused and swirling crowds that I can take. At least for now. The truth is that every conversation takes on the character of a life-lesson. Every conversation takes thought and processing and follow-up. You could read all your life and never get as much in a professional degree as you can get just talking to women on the streets here. They are financial planners, social engineers, government ministers, theologians, philosophers, doctors, scientists, sociologists. They are all doing something to reshape life as we know it so that women can come to know life as men know it – in all its fullness, with all its security, all its opportunity, all its potential. The woman next to me at lunch launched a woman's bank. The woman next to me in line organizes women in barrios in South America to pressure governments into developing sanitation projects in these areas. The woman sitting next to me in the peace tent has written text books for children on the effects of militarism. A woman in the cab with us writes stories about the lack of adoption facilities in Asia and the effects of female infanticide on social structure.

It's an exciting thing, this conference. It is like a second-hand ticking away before the dynamite blows in a match factory. All the poor of the world – colored, landless and female – are rising up out of the slime of the earth to claim their birthrights. It is an age-old conflict, this quest of the deprived for their human inheritance. And in the end, in the long, dark, withering end, the deprived, history records, always, always eventually win.

The NGO Forum

The watchdogs have arrived in Beijing. You can feel it in the air. The Fourth United Nations Conference on Women being held in China these weeks is not one conference. It is two. The first conference, made up of governmental delegates from member countries of the UN, will debate, amend and ratify a Platform for Action designed to make women fully functioning members of the human race. The second conference, the NGO Forum on Women, made up of nongovernmental representatives from women's groups around the world, will monitor and lobby the first one every step of the way.

A sense of urgency pervades without interruption the UN-NGO meeting that stretches for miles through the city of Huairou, China, site of this Fourth International NGO Forum on Women. Delegates, the greater majority of them women, who represent nongovernmental agencies throughout the world, are naming the topics and setting the agendas they want the governments of the world to enforce in behalf of women. NGO's, most of them private and independent agencies which specialize in given areas such as women's health concerns, educational programs or social issues, bring expertise, experience, and passion to topics which might otherwise be overlooked or misunderstood by gov-

ernments. As recently as 20 years ago, for instance, at the time of the First UN Conference on Women in Mexico City, some governments failed to even count women in their national census. Consequently, parliaments and politicians knew how many whales there were in the world in 1975, but country after country did not know how many women it had, or how much education they had received or how much money they made for the work they did.

More significant than the sense of urgency, however, is the feeling of determination that underlies every NGO workshop, every presentation, every event that goes with it. For these groups, words no longer satisfy. No more words will do. "This is a critical conference for women," Chen Muhua, president of the All-China Women's Federation, said in the opening ceremony to the more than 20,000 participants in the NGO Forum in Beijing this week. "What we are demanding now is action to match the words."

United Nations' Conferences on Women, convened in Mexico City, Copenhagen and Nairobi since 1975, gave visibility to the situations of women worldwide. Position paper after position paper asserted their value and the conditions of poverty, oppression, deprivation and danger in which they lived. But, in the end, statistics that describe the actual living conditions of women have changed very little. The needs are apparent. Women are poor, however much they work, in danger, no matter how peaceful they are, treated as an afterthought, whatever their roles. UN studies confirm that women do most of the work, get less of the economic compensation, are routinely deprived of education, are being taken across national borders and sold into bonded labor, domestic service, prostitution and marital slavery, many of them as children, in increasingly larger numbers every year. "Seventy percent of the 1.3 billion people living in poverty in the world are women," Boutros Boutros-Ghali, Secretary-General of the United Nations, reported in his opening statement to the Conference. Twenty-three million refugees and 26 million internally displaced persons in the world, international statistics report, are women. Most of the undernourished of the world, the UN World Health Organization determines, are women for whom access to education and medical care is least available. The situation is clear: What the women at the NGO Forum on Women want now is commitment from the governments of the world to allocate resources and create structures designed to bring women into the world arena as equal and participating partners in the decisions and programs that affect women's lives everywhere. "We are still only objects, not subjects," Helvi Sipila of

Finland, convener of the First UN Conference on Women in Mexico City in 1975, told delegates in Beijing. "How long can women tolerate this situation? We must now make firm plans for the future."

NGO delegates represent groups, hundreds of them, from every point on the ideological spectrum — church Women United and Catholics for a Free Choice, The Kuwaiti Union for Women Associations and The International Movement of Rights and Humanity, The National Abortion and Reproductive Rights Action League and The World Organization of the Billings Ovulation Institute — among hundreds of others. All of them compete equally for the attention of the world and the support of the United Nations delegations, all of them in the name of women's rights and social progress. Plenary presentations stress the role of political participation, the problems posed for women, in particular, by technology and the globalization of the economy, the rise of conservatism and its effects on women, the challenges and opportunities facing women in the media, and the effects of militarization on women. At the same time, two themes in particular surface with special clarity in the hallways and informal discussion sessions at Huariou. The increasing feminization of poverty and violence against women in all its forms emerges consistently as the two main concerns of delegates themselves, whatever their persuasion. Delegates, from developing countries in particular, speak with special passion to the new area of concentration – The Girl Child – which, due to their efforts, has been added to the UN Draft Platform for Action. Workshops on the need to protect small girls from trafficking rings set up to buy females from the Third World for use around the world, including for the procurement of organs for black market medical services, are packed to overflowing day after day.

Finally, undercurrents of the UN Conference on Population and Development held in Cairo in August, 1994 sweep quietly but clearly through the assembly. Attempts by the Vatican and fundamentalist Muslim groups to suppress segments of the Cairo Platform calling for women's reproductive rights is fresh in the memory of NGO groups now active in Beijing. Petitions circulated by "Catholics for A Free Choice," a US reproductive rights group made up of Catholic activists and headed by Frances Kissling, calls for the UN to withdraw the Vatican's "Non-member State Permanent Observer" status. The move to put the Vatican on a par with other religious NGO's attached to the UN, on the grounds that Vatican City is a city-state of much less than half a square mile, rests on the argument that the Vatican does not meet the requirements of a modern state for statehood, and is a religious entity rather than a civil government. Whatever the official response to petitions of this nature, the question is raging here among both NGO and UN delegates alike, and may signal a change in UN-Vatican relations in the future. It may also simply be a sign of things to come in every segment of government and society if women begin to focus both their voices and their votes on aspects of society they regard as repressive of them.

This NGO Forum and UN Fourth Conference on Women is the largest international conference ever convened by the United Nations. It may also, in the long run, be its most important. Until the world is safe for women, for children, for the weak and under-represented everywhere, it is in eternal jeopardy.

So what is the significance of the NGO Forum on Women? To the skeptic, nothing perhaps, but one thing I know for sure: I have seen the face of the world this week and it is not white. It is also not male. It is black and brown and beautiful. It comes in sweeping capes and high turbans, in silks and saris, in corn rows and dangling earrings the size of dinner plates. It comes intelligent, disillusioned and determined. Over 25,000 women have registered for the largest international conference that the United Nations has ever held on one of the least popular subjects the world has every dealt with, "Equality, Development and Peace." It is a meeting of the world's majority, women, about a subject the minority, men, seldom deal with directly. Development and peace the world talks about a great deal, of course. Equality it ignores. In the minds of women here from all over the world, that is exactly why development and peace never happen.

And what does it all mean? It means that women are tired of being poor, tired of being beaten, tired of female infanticide, tired of being talked down to and disregarded, tired of being silent, and tired of bearing daughters who will be the same. It means that it is time for both church and state to take notice. Hillary Clinton comes here this week, heir to Elizabeth Cady Stanton and Eleanor Roosevelt. Gertude Mongella comes, heir to African queens. This week in Beijing thousands of women, in fact, bred a new generation of women. Whatever the social pundits say, there is no sign whatsoever here that feminism is about to dry up and blow away, just one more fad of an errant 20th century. On the contrary. Gertrude Mongella, Secretary General of the Fourth UN Conference on Women, may have said it all in her opening statement to the women of the world: "Millions have placed their trust in us. We must not fail them."

The expectations of the non-governmental delegations to the UN Fourth Conference on Women is clear. All that remains now to be seen is how their governments will answer them. And, have no doubt about it, all the NGO's of the world are watching closely.

The Fourth UN Conference on Women

September 6, 1995

After the US press conference, I shared a cab from the Conference Center to the Hotel 21st Century with a young Scandinavian who worked in Cambodia. He is there for some sort of seminar on wells and water systems. I was meeting Jack and Teresa Wilson and Gail for supper on the Wilsons' last night in Beijing. Tran, the young worker, was one of those '60s types who spend years of their lives working for subsistence wages and drilling wells for poor nations without water. They are clearly the new religious of this century. As long as religious communities do nothing of risk, little of justice and almost nothing to build a new world, the idealism of these types will continue to lead them to social projects instead of to religious communities. If we're lucky, they will lead us religious out of our nice warm security as well. We used to do that kind of risky, insane thing to bring education to barren areas, too. Nuns went into places few people knew existed, and even fewer ever saw, to teach the catechism and prepare an illiterate population for a modern world. Long before public schools got to rural areas, nuns did. They taught in basements and trailers and barns. They lived in farmhouses and cabins and lofts. They laid their bodies down for the next generation. They taught girls when no one felt that girls were worth teaching. Now nuns are going into the ghettos and the soup kitchens and the houses for battered women. They go to Congress to demand resources for the poor and to courts to support exploited women and to public forums to call for justice. But not all. So many are still trapped in the good works of the past, while the Trans of the world do the good works of this one. This conference, I thought, is about what women need to do for women now, in this day and age, in our time. I pray that religious communities will continue to do it or religious communities will become the religious artifacts of the present and the Trans of the world will become its religious.

We had supper on the 25th floor of the hotel, the only people there in fact. It was a wonderful time. I was ready to quit chasing meetings around for awhile and simply to sit down with nice people and put the whole thing in perspective again. Darcy Zotter, a one-time young Pittsburgher and now second director of the US Foreign Service in China, met us for supper and we talked about all the things an American in China needs to know and can't possibly find out in another language. Like Chinese-American relations. Like what it is like to be a woman in the US Foreign Service. Like how long it takes to learn Chinese, and what to do if you are point person for the First Lady of the land, as she is this week. Like the nature of bean curd and the name of a good Chinese wine. Well, everything can't be business.

Tuesday was another one of the wildly uncontrollable wild days that I am beginning to associate with this conference. I am getting very used to simply trying to luck into things around here. It is not good for my ego as a writer, however – notice I do not say "journalist" since that connotes some kind of *paparazzi* fever which I definitely do not have – but, if I am to believe the journalists whom I have met here from the working press of the world, frustration seems to be about par for the course. There is a great deal of criticism, I hear, about the quality of news coverage coming out of this conference. US news agencies seem to be concentrating on Chinese issues and security issues and national political issues rather than on women's issues. They spend time and ink on whether or not Hillary Clinton should come to China – though they said little or nothing about George Bush's presence, who also gave a major speech here the same week and was even paid to do it! They are doing story after story on the harassment of journalists by Chinese security police. They spend endless time on the political implications for US-Chinese relationships if Harry Wu is not released. They are all real questions, of course, but the plight of half the human beings of the world, women, ought to justify a story or two on its own merits, it seems. The content of the conference itself has been almost ignored. It is all just one more demonstration of the trivialization of women. I tried to imagine what kind of stories would be being written if 40,000 men from around the world converged on any one place at any one time to talk to 185 governments about how to change the lives of men in the world. I have a notion that US-Chinese relations would pale into oblivion in about five minutes.

At the same time, in all fairness to the press, it is not easy to get a story here when you can't get into buildings or rooms or meetings or working sessions to follow any idea through to the end. So, because a press pass is almost useless here, I went over to the Beijing Convention Center at about noon to try to get an NGO pass.

I decided to see if I could find an NGO delegate who might be leaving China before the UN Conference closes who would be willing to leave her delegation with me when she goes. After all, the "intention" is to have an open conference here, isn't it — whatever the Chinese attitude toward reporters — so I decided to help them do it. In the end, I found a willing soul with dark curly hair who understood the problem. (Never mind who!) Just like my second-grade teacher said: the angels are everywhere. Now all I have to do is to remember to go in doors monitored by Asian guards for whom "all those whites look alike," rather than Western guards who know blue eyes from brown eyes when they see them.

It was a great day. Not only did I get the NGO pass, I got a backgrounder on the Vatican delegation and a ticket into the Hillary Clinton plenary as well. And that's not even counting a picture with Betty Friedan and a conversation with Bella Abzug and Donna Shalala. It is like tripping over a television set at every corner here. You never know who it is from the national news who will be coming straight at you while you are eating quick-fix noodles out of a plastic container or sitting on a cement wall with your shoes off trying to survive the heat, the lines or the boredom of the place. It was a great day. I am back in business again and things are looking up. I am rolling in clover.

To be in the gallery when Hillary Clinton spoke, to see delegations from all over the world respond with such support for her, to hear her strong and honest words made me proud to be an American woman. "It is indefensible," she said, "that NGO's were not able to participate in this conference." And "It is no longer acceptable to separate women's rights from human rights." There is something about her that smacks of the best in all of us: she is competent, educated, personable, capable, intelligent, brave — a wife and mother who is no less a person for being either. She is the kind of woman I want every girl alive to have the opportunity to be. It was worth the wait for the ticket, worth the pushing and shoving, worth the long day in the sun. None of us lives totally out of our heads. Ideas can carry the spirit only so far. We all live on signs of hope, models of possibility, words of truth.

So, all in all, the day glowed for me. At the same time, I haven't been able to see anybody that I am trying to see: not Mary Ann Glendon, head of the Vatican delegation, not Gertrude Mongella, Secretary-General of the conference, not even Soon Young Yoon, the UN liaison to the NGO Forum, each of whom could give valuable background information to the current foment and pressures. Nobody knows where anybody is or where anybody will be, though, and, if you do find out, the security between you and them is so tight that walking up and saying hello to someone you'd like to talk to becomes one of life's more creative tasks.

Anele, a Dominican sister from the States, "an Israelite in whom there is no guile," came back to the hotel with us for supper, and we ate far too much and talked far too long about far too many depressing things: the church's exclusion of women, the age-old division between lay women and nuns, the disenchantment with the sacraments in a male church. I groaned inwardly at the whole thing. It gets so tiring. Why don't we all just walk away from it en masse? Why don't we? The question is a simple one; the answers are complex. Any church's monopoly on the human soul is no small power, no small oppression. And yet the tradition is ours, too. The spiritual life belongs to us, too. Jesus became flesh, not simply male, we believe. We are the memory of their better theology. It was a long, long conversation that went deep into the evening and caused more anxiety than resolution. But then, that is what this conference is all about – naming the demons, facing them and decrying them for our daughters' sakes.

But good conversations stir the blood. There went my hopes for an early night.

September 6, 1995

Today, I declared a day off for myself. The fact is that I have been going non-stop for weeks and it is beginning to show. So, when I realized this morning how much I would have to rush to make the NGO briefing by 8:00, I just decided to roll over, move slowly and let the day take its own shape. And it did.

First, I checked the e-mail and discovered a letter from Tom Fox, the editor of the *National Catholic Reporter,* saying that my last article had never gotten to the office. I called Erie mmediately and discovered that the article was lost in his office, not in mine, and decided to simply enjoy the conversation since I had now paid for it. After all, it's been a long time since I communicated with more than a computer screen. The church calls it, "O happy fault." I like that idea. It covers every mess I make in life.

We left the room at about noon, had toasted cheese sandwiches and french fries for breakfast (obviously it wasn't breakfast time for them but it was for me), and took off down the street in the relentless Beijing rain. I came home with Chinese chopping knives for Christmas gifts and not much else, but it has been nice for a while to be out of the schools of people that weave and sway back and forth from one conference building to another. The streets are a sea of bicyclers in bright plastic ponchos sweeping down the wide highway five and six abreast. It is the strangest sight. The Chinese have the capacity to be serene in the middle of chaos. They even ride their bicycles in a kind of mesmerizing rhythm. Nobody races ahead. No teenagers terrorize small children and old women by cutting in front of them or slicing around corners or tailgating their way through town. Everybody just gets in line and glides away, in perfect order, in perfect pace.

Today's papers are full of Hillary Clinton's address to the UN Conference and NGO Forum, calling for more accessible NGO participation and abhorring the Chinese policy of forced sterilizations and abortions. The complexity of the subject is beginning to present itself in multiple dimensions. Therapeutic abortions are only one aspect of the subject – and this one most unclear of all to multiple people of good will, who are struggling to arrive at some consensus on the nature of life rather than the question of the moral desirability of abortion to which few, if any, ascribe. Abortion as a birth control method of choice is another consideration, highly debatable and, if we are to believe the polls, highly suspect. But forced abortions as a state population policy are, in the opinion of most, entirely unacceptable under any circumstances. The question of reproductive rights is a matter far more serious than the decision not to have a child. In some parts of the world, it involves the matter of being allowed to have one as well. We have to begin to look at the implications of abortion as social policy. As genocide. As population control. If abortion is legal, can a government abort the citizens it does not want? They do here in this country, they tell us. Tibetans say they are being exterminated this way. But if that becomes the case, maybe Adolph Hitler was simply a warning of worse horrors to come and not the real thing at all. So we are left with a situation where some feminists argue that abortion is essential to the liberation of women, yes, but feminists are also saying here that systems using abortion for population control of whatever kind are the ultimate oppressors of women. "Reproductive rights" is clearly not a one-dimensional concept, and cannot be discussed in a one-dimensional way. People have no trouble whatsoever distinguishing between the moral implications of multiple kinds of wars and warheads, of some kinds of killing as opposed to other kinds of killing. We're going to have to look at this situation with the same kind of acuity. Either life is sacred everywhere, at all times, in every situation or it isn't. Or maybe we should just ask why it is that killing is theologized when men do it and anathematized when women do it?

Minzu Hotel is Chinese, genuinely Chinese. It does not cater to foreigners. All the signs in the lobby leave you with at best a calculated guess about the services of the house. The value of the brochures stops at the pretty pictures, but the warmth and beauty of the place itself makes the step into another culture more than worth the risk. If you go into the coffee shop, three people wait on you at all times. If you want a cab, four drivers put you in the car. If you stop in the hotel boutique, every clerk in the store follows you from item to item, waiting for the slightest indication of interest or need. They smile and smile and run to get you what you want. They try to speak English and garble every attempt, but their English is better than my Chinese, so then they try again. Behind it all is a gentle kind of care, a finesse, a concern that is rare. There is something about the Asian heart that rings true.

At the same time, there is plenty about China that I do not understand, the greatest of which is the dearth of the countryside and the frenzied consumerism of the city. Beijing is full of consumer goods. This is definitely not Communism as we have come to think of it. The hotels are plush; the architecture is modern; the store fronts are full of gold-plated bathroom fixtures; the department stores are slick and packed with high quality Western goods; Gucci and Giorgio and Nina Ricci are featured everywhere and are very much at home here. The place is one large creeper-crane on top of one new high-rise building after another. Finally, I haven't seen a Mao shirt and cap since I came. And yet, there are still

only one million cars for eight million bicycles, with all the bicyclers trying to get cars. Where is progress? What is progress? This
is a Western city with an Eastern heritage. You can't help but
wonder what will happen when they achieve the Westernization at
which they are aiming – to them, to us, to a world hell-bent on
having what we do and hating us at the same time for the rape of
the earth that such "progress" has spawned.

September 7, 1995

Today was a good day. I went to the NGO briefing at 8:00 a.m.
The two experiences – the Forum and the Conference – are beginning to come together now. The things we heard in Huairou now
have echoes here. These NGO delegates want action from the
governments of the world on economic issues. They want the protection of girl-children through international law. They want the
elimination of the gender-gap in education. They want health care
for women. They want protection from abuse. NGO delegates on
every delegation, NGO experts on every issue, track every working group, every amendment, every political compromise and report back to the larger body daily. They keep a running tab on
what items of the Platform for Action are in question, or being
debated, or are in danger of being lost. Then, every day the group
disperses to do more work, talk to more delegates, provide more
materials, go to more hearings with the NGO agenda firmly in
mind. It goes on from early morning until late, late at night. This
is not your average professional convention. This is serious business. This will determine what the family of nations will say that
being a woman is all about. And try to remember that what they
have said in the past has shaped the life of women for generations. As I listened to the reports, I wondered how many people
realize that the laws that governed the legal definition of slaves in
the United States were the very same laws that governed women.
Women weren't treated like slaves; slaves were treated like women.

The US delegation briefing at 12:30 opened up an interesting question. The US delegation stands firmly in support of the
Platform of Action as written but, given the present budget maneuvering in the United States, refuses to promise additional funds to
promote and enable the actions it affirms. Strange. We can give
the men of a nation the tanks they ask for without so much as a

national whimper, let alone a cry of outrage. But we won't give the women of a nation the doctors they need or the education they want because we don't have the money. Not for women. In fact, our politicians get elected to take money away from women and children. At the same time, I was proud of the delegation, too. I could tell that they want to do more. And can't. The Old World lives on.

I gave an interview to Peter Mann, a soft-souled man with beautiful kind eyes, at about 2:00 today on questions I don't even remember right now. I am too talked out to tell one subject from another at this stage. There must be something else to say about all of this, but I do not have the least idea what it is right now except, perhaps, "Enough. Enough. Enough, already. Women have taken enough."

I bought some bamboo fans for Christmas gifts as we walked by some of the tiny shops near the Convention Center. Then we took off for the Silk Market. It was beautiful and disappointing at the same time. The Silk Market consists of blocks of tiny stalls owned by simple people, all reminiscent of the small boutiques in the bazaars of the Middle East, except that here there is a great deal more order in the layout of them. Here you don't have to worry about disappearing into the bowels of a maze of shops and never being seen or heard from again. These tiny little lean-to stalls stand in a long, straight line, and cops are everywhere. I hated to admit it but back there on that dark, cramped street, they brought a warm, secure feeling.

At the same time that it is a quaint and friendly place, it is also a kind of sad place. Almost everything in the market is Western. There are few Chinese styles left. You also get the distinct impression that whatever silk goods exist in China, most of them exist to be exported to the United States. They are catering to the capitalist world and giving up their own culture to do it. I ask you, Rabbi, is that a good thing?

A gaggle of pedicab cyclers crowded around us, trying to get us to hire one of them for the ride back to the hotel. Nothing doing, buddy. Once bitten is an accident; twice-bitten is a terminal disease.

We took a cab to the Lido Hotel to eat in "The Texas Bar and Grill" for a change. The Chinese waiters wear cowboy hats, tall boots, gun belts and checkered kerchiefs around their necks. Somehow or other I had gone to China and wound up at the bottom of Alice-in-Wonderland's rabbit hole. I blinked. Then, I ordered salsa and chips, a baked potato and a piece of meat. Meat and potatoes. Plain and simple. There was something very wonderful about not having what I was eating for supper lost in a mystery of MSG and mixed vegetables that I have never seen before. It was also nice to know what I was eating for a change, much as I have loved the sight and spice of Chinese food. I guess you just get to a point, after days of straining to understand and negotiate and listen and learn, in a foreign land where your psyche needs to rest in the familiar. Well, today I hit it. Food, I have discovered on this trip, says a lot of things: it defines a culture; it creates community; it gives form to hospitality; it brings comfort at a time of confusion. Tonight the name of the game was comfort.

The Vatican Delegation has agreed to meet tomorrow afternoon with any NGO's who might be interested. I'm looking forward to it and I'm dreading it at the same time. Nations come to the conference as one voice among many. The Vatican and other religious groups seem to come with some sort of message from on high, as if most of the messages from on high about slaves and war and Divine Right kings haven't changed over time. Why is it that we can't all just search out the answers together instead of some of us playing at being oracles and the rest of us playing at being blind beggars, spiritual children, moral miscreants? Is this really the way God wanted the Spirit to work in the church?

September 8, 1995

Today is the 43rd anniversary of the beginning of my monastic life. When I entered the Erie Benedictines at the age of 16, I was sure, first of all, that I would never, never do a public thing again and, secondly, that I would certainly never do any more writing. Now I am at a United Nations Conference in China – writing about it. Moral: Don't be too sure of anything, ever. Since the day I said goodbye forever to my mother and father, there's been a Vatican Council that reformed the church, the toppling of a Communist wall that has reformed the world, and the rise of the women's question which is reforming relationships around the globe. And I have been in the middle of all of them. How is such a thing possible?

It was another hectic day at the UN Conference – an NGO briefing and a meeting with the Vatican delegation to the UN.

At the briefing you could feel the pressure beginning to build. These women want a decrease in military spending, and they want a new post for women's issues created at the UN itself, the purpose of which will be to monitor the implementation of this Beijing Platform for Action around the world. Most of all, they want countries to make specific commitments to the Platform. The move to secure national commitments began in Australia. "We thought it only made good sense," the presenter said. Sure, I thought, good sense. But since when did good sense have anything to do with the way institutions treat women? I admired the women for trying. "NGOs are the soul of us all," Bella Abzug said. Bella comes in a wheelchair to these meetings on the other side of the world, and when she appears I can feel my heart tighten. It is women like Bella Abzug who gave their lives that this moment could come. How do you say thank you for something like that? Anne Morrow Lindbergh said, "One can never pay in gratitude. One can only pay in kind somewhere else in life." I must keep remembering this. There is some woman somewhere who is waiting for me to do the same for her as Bella has done for all of us.

One of the most important things in life is to remember not to let your education interfere with your learning. We began quite consciously today to fit the cultural into the schedule as surely as we did the conference. So, the day was a full one, yes, but in between sessions, quite unaware of the implications, we got into a cab and went to Yonghi Gong Lamasery. Yonghi Gong, an active Buddhist monastery of 80 Yellow Hat monks, is a sect of Buddhism much the same way that Franciscans and Benedictines are orders of the Roman Catholic church. The experience touched me to the center of my soul. One temple after another unfolds the mystery of Buddhist spiritual life until, in the fifth one, the seeker is confronted with a 75-foot statue of the Buddha that is carved out of a single sandalwood tree. Think of it. Seventy-five feet is almost eight stories high. You start at the Buddha's feet and you look up, and up, and up until your head is back against your neck and you are swaying on your feet. I couldn't help but remember a Buddhist story I'd heard. Once upon a time, the story tells, a very learned priest went to the monastery to receive instruction from a monk who was world-renowned for giving profound spiritual guidance. "I am seeking a revelation that will change my life," he said. "What should I do?" "Well," the guru said, "Go out into the courtyard, put your hands up, tilt your head back to heaven and I promise you that a life-changing revelation will come to you." About an hour later, the monk found the scholar-priest standing in the foyer of the monastery, dripping wet and obviously agitated. "And what revelation came to you, dear priest?" the Holy One said. "Revelation?" the priest fumed. "It was pouring down rain and I was standing there with my arms up and my head back. I felt like a perfect fool!" "Well," the monk said, "That's a pretty important revelation for only the first day." I stood there aware of all the petty moments of my monastic life and looked up and up and up – and felt like a perfect fool.

There, in the middle of Beijing, we were plunged into instant peace and harmony and beauty and silence. Call the whole thing false in a Communist world if we must, but this monastery is nevertheless the reminder of things spiritual in an atheistic state. When this state dies, and it will, Buddhism will rise again out of the soil of this silence. For me, it was a call back to the deepest part of the Benedictine tradition, the one that grounds me when all of this activity becomes disorienting, the core of Benedictinism – the contemplative, the centered. I walked through the five halls, from one incense burner to another, from one set of Buddha to another with respect and a kind of secret solemnity. This was more my home than the UN would ever be, more my desire than all the train trips and meetings in the world, more my element than anywhere else in which I find myself over and over again. These have been wrenching years in so many ways, but one thing has never changed in me – I have a great desire to sink into the soulfulness of life and never come out, and I come out precisely because I have spent my life searching for its soulfulness. Figure that one out if you can.

The meeting with the Vatican delegation was a strange mixture of human commitment and ecclesiastical distance. The women on the delegation did all the talking. The priests sat there with their arms folded, a little chagrined, I thought, because it was totally clear that the women in the room were no more impressed with what they thought than they would have been with the ideas or philosophical convictions of any other man about the role and place of women. They didn't have to worry, however. The women on the delegation have been carefully chosen to reflect the Vatican position, to raise no contrary opinions, to entertain few questions and to ignore the ones that will not go away. There were clearly very few ideological problems on this delegation, if any. Which is not to say that the women were not perfectly sincere. I know that because I remember when I was just as unquestioning as they of what passed itself off as religious certainties. Only after years of resistance did I realize that prejudice and parochialism, magic and misunderstanding of some basic truths of life can infect religion, too – like were blacks fully human and did indulgences buy people out of purgatory and did non-Catholics go to heaven?

People asked the delegation what specific commitments the Vatican intended to make to the Platform for Action and the concept of the empowerment of women in decision-making positions in the church itself. But the "answers" were at best assurances, a kind of evangelical repetition of the "trust us" argument. The church had already issued a statement committing all of its educational institutions around the world to the advancement of women, they said. Exactly what would be defined as "the advancement of women" went unexplained in today's discussion, but promised to get attention in times to come, however, if the document being shaped here gets any kind of universal approbation at all. I spoke to Mary Anne Glendon, the head of the Vatican delegation, before we left. The best thing that has happened to her as a person in this process, she says, is "the wonderful people on the delegation, – the best in the world – and the liturgies in the group." She is clearly a good woman, a true believer. I will send her some materials on contemporary spirituality, maybe even a copy of my own book, *Wisdom Distilled from the Daily,* in order to make a personal connection. I'm sure she is not as much a chauvinist patsy as some people say – she is, after all, a very successful professional – and I am not nearly as much of a heretical radical as the rest of the people say. That ought to make for interesting contact.

I am spending more money than I would do under normal situations, but this is not a normal situation. It's impossible for non-Chinese to get around this city unless you take a taxi. I mean, how do you read the bus signs? Food is phenomenally expensive in the hotels, at least for foreigners whom the Chinese cheerfully admit they gouge, and since we have no way to go anywhere else late at night when the meetings are over, we are a captive clientele. Now, to make matters worse, we are all realizing that we have been in Beijing for days and have yet to see anything more than the Convention Center. It's a nice convention center, but it could just as easily be in Chicago as in Beijing. So, now we're all trying to get cheap tours to all the hot spots – the Great Wall, the

Ming Tombs, the Forbidden City, Tiananmen Square – and this so-called Communist government is not a bit embarrassed to charge everything the traffic will bear for the privilege. Every ticket booth has two windows: one for Chinese, one for foreigners. Every ticket booth has two prices, in other words, one for them and one for us. The nice thing about Chinese Communism is that it is unabashed capitalism. I am groaning at every bill but laughing about it, all at the same time. Who wouldn't bilk a capitalist? After all, that's the name of the capitalist game, isn't it?

I would love to crawl under the covers and just die for a while, but that is not how you get from here to home. I have packed my suitcase full of small gifts. Now it is time to start through the huge pack of papers that I've accumulated in the course of these weeks. I can't possibly get all of it out of here. I came in a stewardess case, remember? And it was full to the gills coming. Something has to go – clothes, gifts or papers. I need the clothes; I wore myself out looking for gifts. I need the information in the papers. This is going to be a tough one.

It is Friday night and the day of the Moon Festival that celebrates the fall harvest. Beijing is out in the streets in force. Tiananmen Square was a crush of people. They are dancing on every street corner and, down the street from our hotel in front of the Hall of Minorities, there was a huge outdoor program of ethnic dances and songs. We walked down and joined the Chinese audience that was pressing against the fence to watch the show. It was a peaceful, silent group. The huge marble building with the high pagoda tower was outlined in lights against the black night. The full moon was bright. Fathers carried small children on their shoulders. It was a perfect night.

I realized as we walked back to the hotel that there had been no charge for the performance. The production was packed with young families and old couples, teenagers and adults. Cultural events are commonly free in Communist nations. I wish I could say the same thing about a country where phenomenal wealth has been built up by commerce and technology but which finds it close to impossible to subsidize the arts.

September 9, 1995

Today was perfect, too. Or almost perfect. We took a private tour to the Ming Tombs and the Great Wall. The young student guide spoke perfect English. He is an acupuncturist who is now intent on studying in Japan. He applied acupressure to my injured finger as we drove, in fact, and I bent it for the first time in 10 days. He is also quite an entrepreneur. We paid him about 390 Yuan – $50 each – for the day. Ah, well. The average Chinese makes about $25.00 a week. You can't go to Japan on that. And acupuncturists don't come cheap these days either.

The Great Wall was a timely meditation. If it proves anything at all – besides the sheer intrepid abilities of these people – it proves that we simply cannot defend ourselves from one another. We must learn to live together. I am convinced that the Chinese were certain when they built the Wall that they were then and forever totally secure. It was, at the peak of its development, over 7000 miles long and wide enough for a phalanx of 10 infantrymen to walk it abreast. But the wall was breached three times. Just as nuclearism has been breached. Just as national borders everywhere have been breached. I stood at the highest point of the wall and watched it snake across the mountains for miles, and felt the full futility of militarism.

We had a great lunch. The food was not only good, it was abundant. We had dish after dish of the best food China could offer in the simplest kind of restaurant you could imagine. I marvel at the level of culture in a country that is balancing precariously between the 18th and the 21st centuries. And I ought to know. Today I had both. The food was 21st-century quality. The bathroom they took me to at the same place was 18th-century – if that. The hole in the floor of an open stall was one thing; the three naked girls taking a shower under the leaking pipe directly in front of it was entirely another. I had a choice: I could either die of shock or go numb. At the time, numbness was the only acceptable option.

We stopped at a cloisonné factory on the way home, and that education alone was worth the price of the day. Tiny women made tiny designs on copper pots with intense precision. Beauty is such a fantastic thing. It brought tears to my eyes. At the same time, I ached for a process that had been reduced to an assembly-line exercise. I was sure that these same women had put these same curlicues of copper and these same syringefuls of paint on these same pieces for years. They sat on small wooden stools, bent almost double, in bad light, and daubed and pasted, daubed and pasted their lives away. It was tedious work and it was beautiful work, but it was also boring work, not creative work now at all.

Tomorrow morning we will go to the Cathedral, the government church, for Mass and then off to see more of Beijing. It is a schizophrenic culture – great gentility and great repression, ancient culture and new economy, Asian manners and Western businesses. The street below the Great Wall is lined with private vendors, and with Baskin-Robbins and Kentucky Fried Chicken, as well. Tell me that the world isn't one. . . .

September 10, 1995

Sunday. Mass day. So, where to go to church in a Buddhist country? Correction: in an atheist country. I have not been able to make contact with the underground church – and besides, I'm curious. Is the "national" Chinese church Chinese, Catholic or Communist in its style and emphasis? So, we headed off for "The Southern Cathedral," The church of the Immaculate Conception of the National Catholic church. It was about 10:45. It seemed so sensible: Sleep in, take the edge off all these early meetings. Relax. I mean, what Catholic church doesn't have an 11:00 a.m. Mass on Sunday? This one.

We got there just as the 10:00 a.m. English Mass was leaving out, and a swarm of nuns recognized me, stopped to talk about the liturgy for a few minutes and then swept me off "to have tea with the bishop." The fact is that there was no 11:00 a.m. Mass, so tea with the bishop seemed the only church thing to do.

China has more than 10 million Christians, four million of them Catholics attached to 4000 national churches. The Catholics are served by 1200 priests, 2000 active sisters and 70 Bishops. How many Catholics there are in "the underground church," the church loyal to Rome and unrecognized by the Chinese government, is anybody's guess, but this one clearly deserves attention on its own. The conversation had a ring of both theological and political tension to it. Of the 40 students in the Beijing diocesan seminary, six are students in Roman Catholic seminaries in the United States. I got the distinct impression that this was not a church in apostasy; this was a church in waiting. Their political ties with Rome are in abeyance; their liturgical ties are in some dimension, at least, in question; their sense of cultural inde-

pendence is clear, but the tradition goes deep in them nevertheless.

Bishop Michael Fu Tieshan opened the floor immediately to
questions and made two points clear about the nature of Chinese
Catholicism: First, that Rome lost China when Rome insisted that
the Chinese take "Christian" names and refused to allow ancestor
veneration. Secondly, he was very clear about the fact that Catholicism in China had to be Chinese and not Roman. "Rome has
problems with that," he said. "But it will be worked out," he
added with that sly smile the Chinese give you when they know
something you don't know. "What is the status of women in
China?" women wanted to know. "Abhorrent," he said. "We must
have education for women and more women in public positions."
I tried to imagine whether or not we would have gotten that same
answer from most Western bishops. "How did Catholic couples in
China deal with the state one-child policy?" we asked. "It is very
difficult to support a child in China," he pointed out firmly. "We
call for natural birth control," the Bishop said, and then added
slowly and pointedly, "but it is difficult for them." The answer
gave a social nuance to what in Rome is a moral absolute. Here
was a church that intended to keep its culture and resist Roman
centralization. The point stood: The Chinese were Catholics, not
Roman. Furthermore, they were Chinese first of all.

The conversation with a bishop who was asking the same
questions, implying the same problems in the church that most of
the rest of the world does, set off a real firestorm in me. How
much church unity was too much unity? When did unity become a
stifling, ritualistic uniformity? What is the difference between spiritual adulthood and membership in a church? Did Christianity
doom a person to intellectual childhood all their lives – the you-
do-this-because-I-said-so kind? What is the difference between faith
and law? And whose law are we talking about anyway? Who arbi-
trates all of this? And more important than that, maybe, is how is
it done? By fiat? By consensus? By custom? By tradition? By synod?
By pope? I left the place knowing that all the authority questions
in the world had come home to the church. I also left understanding a little better what is really going on in government as
well. It's not simply a struggle between Democrats and Republi-
cans anymore. It is a struggle over who gets the power and for
what purpose and whom does it serve. It is a crossover moment

in history. And women are in the center of it, its goad, its fire-brand, its measure.

Esther, the Presbyterian woman minister from Switzerland, and Pat, who had arranged the conversation with the bishop as part of an in-depth series on Catholicism in China, stayed afterwards to talk awhile. Then one of the Chinese sisters walked the four of us to the seafood restaurant on the corner for lunch. She did all the talking and left us there. I knew I was out of my element when I saw the tank of snakes next to the tank of lobsters in the foyer, and the waiter brought the fish we ordered to the table still flapping in his hand. I kept my eyes down and stuck with the duck.

It was almost 3:00 p.m. when we took off in pedicabs going different directions. The ride down Chang 'an Jei, the 10-lane main street of Beijing, in a pedicab is not an experience for the faint-hearted. Beijing boasts very few traffic lights, and traffic – cars and buses and trucks and bicycles – simply weave in and out of crowded lanes in random fashion. Making a left-hand turn from a right-hand lane in front of double-decker buses and dodging screaming taxis careening around corners defies my idea of a quiet drive on a peaceful Sunday afternoon. That doesn't mean that it wasn't fun. Here we were, two white women, pedaling past half of Beijing who were also pedaling. Fathers pedaled wives and babies, old men pedaled charcoal briquettes, young men pedaled heavy carts of vegetables. This, I thought, might be the real Beijing. In a city of one million cars and eight million bicycles, we had finally joined the right crowd. Marco Polo, eat your heart out.

We cycled around Tiananman Square and up to the main bridge of The Forbidden City, a distance of about two miles from where we'd begun. Then Chinese capitalism took over again. The driver charged us 100 yuan or about $13.00 for the privilege of being scared to death in traffic. A taxi would have cost about $2.00, a bus would have cost a nickel. We had never paid over 185 yuan or about $20 to go the entire 40 miles to Huairou. Ah, how quickly these Chinese learn the fine art of charging what the traffic will bear.

Gail was in shock, more disconcerted than I'd ever seen her. She tried to talk the guy out of it, but a cast of thousands had already crowded around to see the circus. It was getting embarrassing. For my part, I was willing to pay just to get out of the middle of the street. Gail muttered all the way into the Forbidden City. Not about the amount – all things considered, the amount was not much worse than most things Western – but about the blatant exploitation of the thing. Me, I was just glad he didn't call a cop. Wisdom is experience culled for its learnings. The wisdom of this one? Easy: never get into a pedicab in Beijing unless you have negotiated the price first and signed a contract to that effect before a Justice of the Chinese Supreme Court. Otherwise, I promise you, you lose.

Worse, we were too late. After all that, the Forbidden City was closed. Maybe the lesson we had already learned was enough "cultural experience" for the day. I went back to the hotel to write out what was going on in my soul – the struggle of women with male governments. But all the while I remembered a church that had become independent of Rome, and a nation with a culture that predated Rome, and women who were intent on changing the world. Suddenly Rome did not seem so much of an obstacle. And I smiled to myself.

We stayed in the hotel for the rest of the day and ate pizza out of a Pizza Hut box and went to bed early for a change. Maureen called from Erie to tell me that there was only one week of this long excursion left. The call was quick, but long enough to help me reach out and touch the rest of the world for a moment. It was a good feeling. This has been an immersion, a bubble, a kind of time warp on wings. Someplace days are normal and life is not one long struggle to understand how to tell taxi drivers to stop at the next corner.

September 11, 1995

I did one of those quick computer checks in the morning to see if there was anything new, and discovered that I couldn't get on line at all. My Compuserve program had hung up and there was no dislodging it. So much for being able to reach out and touch the real world. I was now on the other side of the world without a lifeline. What a funny people we have become. Distance disappears with telephone lines and becomes immense without them. I remembered another story: "Once upon a time, if people missed a stagecoach they just settled down to wait for the next one to come by in a month or two. Now, Americans get excited if they miss one section of a revolving door." So, I settled down.

Anyway, with an article due in hours I had no way to send it. The nice thing about this meeting is that you can't call it dull.

Every single day something happens that you don't expect, can't fix and didn't anticipate. Isn't that fun? It's called living on the edge and learning to enjoy it.

We went up to the Conference Center for the NGO briefing. Every day the tension gets a little higher. Today there were two issues in question. The first was the use of the word "universal" as a modifier of the term "human rights." What in heaven's name was the problem, I wondered? Why would anyone want to take such a thing out? Weren't we trying to make the point that human rights were the same everywhere and not to be abrogated by anybody? Malta, Iran, Libya, Honduras, Guatemala and the Vatican were opposed, the reporter said. I winced a little.

The second issue caused a stir throughout the room. The declaration of rights regardless of sexual orientation – the notion that civil and human rights could not be abrogated on the basis of sexual orientation – had made it through early readings of the document. The discussion would be continued, the reporter told the group, but so far so good. Women wrote furiously, a few smiled, some raised their eyebrows in disbelief. "The chip," the woman next to me said aloud. "Ah hah," I thought. "So that's it. They leave this statement in until they're making the final compromises. Then the gay community gets sacrificed for the sake of the final consensus. The If-you-put-this-in, we'll-take-this-out game. It's strange how easy it is to forget how politics works when you are operating out of ideals instead.

I went down to the computer room for help they couldn't give me and then to the press room to refine the article and print it out so that I could fax it. Joaquin Navarro-Valls, Vatican Press Secretary, came while we were there to give the regular Vatican interview, but didn't say much that was new. Except one thing. The sexual questions were not Vatican questions, he insisted. They are the obsession of the press. That must be the new Vatican approach to the question. Mary Ann Glendon said it, too. It makes me wonder why we're so intent, then, on decrying birth control and masturbation in official documents if those things aren't as important as the press, apparently, has led us to believe that the church believes. Maybe the only answer to the confusion is to cancel the daily paper. Some of this maneuvering gets funny if you stay with it long enough.

I faxed the article to Erie through my own fax program which, despite the breakdown in Compuserve, is still intact. Intricate but intact. Then, we got a cab and went to the Temple of Heaven where Confucian order and Buddhist serenity lift the soul to heights that crowded, dirty, congested city streets and technological wizardry can never achieve. These places are sanctuaries in the midst of the tumult that we call modern living. You can't help but wonder why we ever traded one for the other.

At Justine's, the restaurant in the Jinggua Hotel, a harpist played while we ate, and then a string quartet did modern ballads, "Loch Lomond, Havah Nagilah," a whole list of songs you had to be 60 to know. Being 50 years behind may be the only way to live.

September 12, 1995

Today I saw two worlds come together in one long human clang. We had breakfast, fresh rolls and coffee at "The Vie de France." And there, sitting in the tiny little table next to us in turned-around baseball caps and "Johnies" T-shirts, sat a crowd of young college students from St. Joe, Minnesota, who know me from their class reading list and seemed to take for granted the fact that we would all be in Beijing together. Tell me again how large the world is? When I was a kid, I never expected to leave town, let alone Pennsylvania. Now young people consider world travel a given, meet you in Beijing and talk to you about things you said before they were born. I was happy – and proud – to see them. They were wholesome, straight-thinking young people. Maybe the world will someday be too small a place to destroy itself, thanks to generations like them.

We spent the afternoon in "The Forbidden City," the 250-acre wonder of the world that rivals the Pyramids and The Great Wall of China. Built in the 15th century, it was the home of 24 emperors from 1420 to 1911, when the last one abdicated in the face of rising Communist or republican pressure. As a piece of architecture, it dwarfs anything I have ever seen anywhere in the world. It occurred to me that I might have even been a little harsh in my evaluation of Ceausescu in Romania. Of all the megalomaniacs, these dynasties may have been the biggest of them all. But they paid a personal price for the privilege. The palace was closed to all commoners and foreigners. That meant that the people of the city could not go through the property for any reason whatsoever. They had to walk around the place to do their business. That must have been difficult for them. It also meant, however, that the Emperor himself was trapped in a grandiose prison all his life, seeing no one, going nowhere. The thought of it stopped me. What price privilege? What price the smallness of power? On the other hand, I thought to myself, we all create prisons of our own making, don't we? We live in them all our lives. We cut ourselves off from anything outside ourselves, and our worlds become smaller all the time as a result. The only difference between us, perhaps, is that these people demonstrated their psychological entrapment in their architecture itself. We spend our lives trying to hide ours. There were lessons aplenty to be learned here.

At the same time, the emperors all believed in spending hours in their formal garden, a spiritual maze of pagodas, old trees, rock mountains, incense burners and cement terraces. It was a good lesson, too, I thought. We all need a garden in the midst of our lives but most of us, especially Americans, I'm afraid, never take enough time from our work to rest our minds. You wonder who, in the end, really has the greater culture and longer-lasting achievements – the civilizations who spend their time on commuter trains or the civilizations that walk in gardens.

At the same time, I was overwhelmed by the incredible beauty of it all. The symmetry, the lacquers, the colors, the perfect balance and vast, vast spaces expand the soul to the breaking point. I must go home and see "The Last Emperor" again. I cried the last time I saw it. I can't even imagine what it will do to me this time now that I have seen the artificial splendor of one world and the reality of the one that supplanted it. How is that the 20th century could possibly have contained both? I am beginning to think that this century has been one of the major fissures of all human history. Nothing like it preceded it and nothing like it will follow.

Going in to the Forbidden City, I bought a small bag from a small stall, bargained for a good price and then negotiated to leave it at the booth until we came out of the City, rather than carry it around with me the whole long day. The keepers of the booth smiled and nodded and smiled again at me as I paid them the money and handed them back the bag, this time with my name on it. Acres later, hours later, we found ourselves at the gates at the other end of the City walls. I turned around, looked back over the building tops, calculated the distance from where I was standing back to the stall at the entrance gates and made a quick decision: Goodby, bag. Under no conditions was I walking all the way back through that sweep and stretch of land and buildings to get it. No wonder they were so willing to bargain. No wonder they smiled.

These days in Beijing have been a microcosm of life for me – a study in contrasts, a teeter-totter of experiences that ranged from the very difficult to the very exhilarating, the very exciting to the very sobering. I am, for instance, looking at some of the world's most tragically illiterate women on the streets of Beijing. At the same time, I am looking as some of the most professionally literate women in the world in the Conference Center across town. All these women are in the same city at the same time. They are all watching one another, evaluating one another, talking about one another. They are all trying to make the world a better place for their daughters. They are each of them from incredibly different worlds and the same world at the same time. It is like a human face split down the middle and painted a different color on each side. Only together are they womanhood, part of it in the light, the rest of it in darkness yet.

We left by the North Gate to get a taxi back to the Minzu. The Emperors may have been carried everywhere they went in the Forbidden City but I had to walk it. I had all the culture my legs could take for one day. A pedicab offered to take us for 30 Yuan, about $4.00 – the same distance as we had been taken by pedicab on Sunday for 100 yuan, about $13.00, but we are smarter now. We took a cab for 15 yuan, about $2.00. We're learning how to live in this town, and it is just about time to go home.

The Korean Restaurant next door to the hotel served a great meal tonight, but they wanted to do it in about 20 minutes. At 9:00, all the help ran out the door with mincing little Asian steps, and two guards and the manager watched us in sullen silence, arms folded, from afar. There is nothing like it to dampen the appetite. I had memories of my mother waiting in the same position for me to finished my cold mashed potatoes. This may be one of the major cities of the world, but they live on an agrarian schedule. They roll up the streets very early around here. It is an urban population with a rural soul.

Strolling home, we remembered again that "Communism" is only a generic term. This is not the Communism they described in the West. This one is lively and happy and bent on a neon future. Have no doubt about it: If human energy and determination have anything to do with success, they are going to get it – Communism or no Communism. The question that plagues me is this: Is this really "Communism" in the economic sense of the term or is this simply totalitarianism in the political sense of the term? Maybe we will only know that in 10 years, when progress in China makes isolationism impossible and totalitarianism anachronistic.

September 13, 1995

Today was a breathless kind of day. I was up early and on my way to the Beijing International Convention Center (the BICC to cab drivers) at about 7:10 a.m. The briefing was at 8:00 a.m., and I had an interview scheduled with Geraldine Ferraro at 10:00. I wanted to be there on time, but life here does not admit of many certainties.

First, the briefing was longer than usual. Economic and environmental issues take high priority among the NGO's. Money that goes into economically undeveloped nations does not go to women. Nor are women being educated to become part of the projects that funding groups will subsidize. Most of all, these women are angry about the continued devaluation of women's work in the home. It's an interesting moment. All these professional feminists, all these feminist professionals, stand squarely behind the valuation of domestic work as part of the GNP. We count the work of men who take time off to think, and pay them for it, and call it a sabbatical! We don't count the work of women who raise the next generation of the world. Now where are the reactionaries who can argue that feminists are opposed to motherhood, that this is an anti-family document? I felt the frustration of years of criticism and set my sights on the road ahead – however long it takes.

I left the briefing racing to be on time for my interview with Geraldine Ferraro and wondering how a woman like her maintains this pace, stays in this mix of international meetings year after year and goes on functioning with equanimity and civility. These positions require a certain quality of soul.

The United States Information Office, where Ambassador Ferraro agreed to meet with me, was in another building. The term "another building" here is a euphemism for "miles away." I groaned. There was a labyrinth of crowded escalators and security checks and service corridors and packed parking lots and slow elevators between her and me. It was good material for a B-movie but it was not my idea of how to center yourself for a serious conversation. Forget it. At a time like this, everything gets collapsed, truncated, overlooked – and accepted. Anyway, however unraveled I might have been by that time, Geraldine Ferraro was not. In the middle of the nations of the world, under time constraints that were major, on her way now to another meeting, she was poised, concentrated and fully focused.

We walked across the parking lot from the USIS Office to her delegation meeting together, talking as equals, openly and honestly. She turned my press badge upside down and simply walked me into the delegation meeting where I did not qualify to be so that our conversation could be natural and concentrated.

Geraldine Ferraro is a cultivated, proficient and courageous woman who, having once campaigned for the vice-presidency of the United States with then-presidential candidate Fritz Mondale, is now US Ambassador for Human Rights to the UN. I didn't ask her the regular background questions. I asked her for answers to the ones that were bothering me at the time. Forget the journalistic protocol. This was a woman who was willing to talk to you as if you were a human being, and this was the chance of a lifetime. What does this global, hodge-podge of a world look like to people who are sitting in the middle of it? I wanted to know about women's rights, the role of the Vatican, the struggle over reproductive rights and the ultimate effectiveness of this conference. She was firm and she was clear, a rare mixture for a politician.

Why had the term "universal" human rights been written out of the document, I asked.

The committee had eliminated the word "universal" as a modifier of the term "human rights," she said, because "all human rights are universal." True in the philosophical sense, of course, but there was another reason as well. "Some countries," she went on, "fear that the term implies that someone can impose an arbitrary set of 'rights' on everybody else, simply by getting most people to agree that the rights they espouse are universal ones. The problem lies in concern for sovereignty, not rights."

Should the Vatican be a member of the UN, I asked her?

"The Vatican," she says, "brings spiritual values to the international conversation and is no more a religious voice than the theocratic Muslim nations, who are also speaking from a religious perspective, or the secular states, who are areligious and who speak from an ethical and moral position but not from a religious one." We need all those perspectives, she implied.

What did she want to say to women in general and to Catholic women in particular? She sounded firmer on this subject than on any of the others. "Catholic women who have been raised to see motherhood as paramount can become very intolerant of other women," she said gently. "Especially if they have good husbands. We have to take a closer look at what is happening to women in the rest of the world. Catholics need to realize," she said, "that the women's issue is broader than the reproductive rights issues and even broader than the very narrow definition of 'family' to which we are accustomed. There are other kinds of families that need to be protected: parentless families, single-parent families, extended families, non-traditional families. We can't use Catholic positions on those subjects to justify rejection of Catholic social postures on poverty and human rights and justice."

The responses were very pointed, very thought-provoking. They raised important ideas with which the human community, the religious community, must deal. Clearly "reproductive rights" has something do with the right to have children as well as the right not to have children. "Family" means multiple things to multiple cultures. To deny people in poverty the resources they need to put bread on their tables because we disapprove of their positions on moral issues is its own kind of immorality. And a very uncatholic one at that, if the social teachings of the church are to be weighed at all. The effect of this conference was "to set forth goals," she said, by which the family of nations would be measured on its treatment of women. And measure we must.

I found Geraldine Ferraro strong and balanced and very, very human. She was also very free, very ethically sophisticated, very shaped by her own tradition and experiences and training. She had a conscience, a Catholic conscience, and it was very clear about what she was doing and why. She had long ago gone beyond religion to the kind of goodness that sees beyond culture, beyond religion, beyond country to other kinds of goodness in other kinds of people as well as her own. I got an impression of commitment rather than politics, and I liked what I saw. She has an international heart. I remembered standing in front of the dais in the city park in Erie when she campaigned for the vice-presidency in 1988. I was younger then, but I knew that she represented more than the government for me. She represented what women could and would someday become. Unless, of course, God is a masochist who made women with brains only so that they could be eternally frustrated by not being able to use them.

The NGO delegates to the Conference are not, in most part, happy with the Conference at this point. There is a great deal of anxiety about losing some of the positions that were gained in Cairo on population and reproduction issues. It is hard to know at this point who is right, what is really going on, how people will vote in the end and whether or not we are now into a reductionism that renders the document international pablum or real political clout. Everyone you talk to puts a different interpretation on the material. Actually, they're probably all correct.

Walking back and forth across this giant complex makes for an experience in its own right. Everything takes more effort than daily life demands under normal circumstances. Committee meetings are buildings apart. Coffee is floors away. Press conferences are shifted from place to place. The cab stand is three blocks on the other side of the center. Yet, how could it possibly be any different? There were over 30,000 delegates at the NGO Forum, and there are 17,000 delegates here at the UN Conference, and anything that holds that many people in separate rooms is bigger than anyone can manage.

We had lunch in a hotel dining room, and paid $27.00 for two toasted cheese sandwiches, french fries and a fruit plate. It costs to starve around here.

At 3:00 p.m. I went to the Caucus for Indigenous Women, the invisible and unheard women of the conference. It was a gentle and painfully poignant meeting. The chairwoman, an American Indian, opened the session with a prayer. "Let us each ask our ancestors, the women who have gone to the other side, to ask the Creator to lead us and guide us to make decisions for the good of the children." The prayer gave me pause in itself. "For the good of the children." I couldn't help but wonder how many decisions that criteria would cancel in US politics, in US business, in US families. I had heard about the Tenth Generation Rule – the Indian idea that every decision must be made in the light of its effect on 10 generations hence. Before this meeting I had been foolish enough to believe that the idea was a lovely but quaint relic of the past.

The indigenous women in the room came from Canada, Greenland, Ecuador, Asia, Brazil, the Pacific Islands, Peru, the Russian Federation and the Indian Reservations of the United States.

They have lost their lands, their government, their property rights, their resources and even their identities as peoples, as nations, within the borders of other nations. "We are called Indian Nations," one woman observed, "but not dealt with on those terms." Now they are arrayed against all the multinational powers of the world. Large corporations come into indigenous areas, milk the women of the tribes for their knowledge of herbs and animals, ransack the lands of them, package the information and the balms and pocket the profits. They leave behind not even so much as a thank you. These women are struggling valiantly for bargaining power and remuneration for the "intellectual property" they have lost, but who will listen? Who will care? The room stank with pathos. I felt like I was watching an ant struggle with an elephant. I was on the ant's side, but the elephant couldn't have cared less.

We went to the Friendship Store after the meeting and got a few small last-minute gifts and our signature seals, a very ancient Chinese artifact for sealing letters and signing documents, and, oh yes, a new dufflebag for $10. There is no doubt about it now: I will definitely not be able to go home in a single suitcase. Someday I have to quit accepting samples and picking up books everywhere I go. I also have to quit trying to do my Christmas shopping in strange countries. Someday surely I will simply resort to hankies and ties. Someday surely. But not yet. After hours of haggling over quality and prices, we went next door to the Pizza Hut for supper. It was a contrast of major proportions. In the Friendship Store, English was at a premium. In the Pizza Hut, it was the *lingua franca* of every young waiter. Every one of them is studying the language of international business. Everyone of them is on his way to somewhere else. China is westernizing at great speed. What's more, I am happy to say, quality control is alive and well in Beijing and, as much as I hate to admit it in the land of Peking Duck and fresh, flapping fish, the pizza tasted like home. I loved the stuff.

A priest member of the Vatican Delegation, a monsignor active in the Vatican's pro-life movement, called our room tonight to ask whether or not it was true that the Peace Train had been subsidized by the Planned Parenthood Association. I laughed out loud at the thought. I got a little angry, too. If there is anything that does not help a difficult conversation, it is paranoia. The Peace Train was a peace train. Its concern was people everywhere. It went under no political banner, it had no particular agenda except reconciliation and equality. I don't even know, nor do I care, how all the women on that train felt about Planned Parenthood or Pro-life programs or Pro-Choice legislation or anything else. One thing I do know, however: There were some of each on that trip, I bet, but in no way did that group come into Beijing with a single-subject legislative initiative in mind. I suppose I should be thankful that at least he called to ask. So few people do. They just assume things and make war on the basis of their singular assumptions.

September 14, 1995

The Conference is winding to a tight and nervous close. This morning's briefing was tense and disturbingly vague. Some of the women want to write their own alternative declaration. They find the UN declaration weak, vague and basically meaningless. These people mean business. They didn't come to Beijing for poetry. They came for specific results.

Sometimes it sounds as if the Platform has the universal support it will take to change the world overnight. At other times, it sounds as if the world – and the women's movement – is splitting apart at the seams right in front of our faces. The briefings have been one long cry for mutual support. Handicapped women asked for access. Tibetan women asked for freedom from China. Indigenous women asked for intellectual property rights. Women in war zones pleaded for pressure groups to decry the militarization of the world. Lesbians begged for protection from civil discrimination. If you cannot help us, every group entreated the assembly, at least do us no harm. Don't barter us away, in other words. Don't sell out our rights for yours.

I took a long set of notes to give foundation to my last article, talked to people from the various caucuses and checked on the schedule for the last day. If it is the last day. No one can be sure whether or not the Platform will be approved tomorrow until this day is over. The rumor, of course, is that the delegations from Muslim countries and the Vatican will register a series of reservations, despite all the compromises and negotiations made in their behalf to this point. Women are very angry about the whole thing. After all, they argue, we have weakened the document considerably in deference to them and they are not going to accept it anyway. It is a point. My own opinion is that if groups resist this worldwide movement like that, they will simply isolate themselves even more on the international scene and go down in history as shortsighted obstructionists. My sadness is the sin against religion that people commit in the course of playing God. How is it that we can blame God's will for the oppression of women? Doesn't that say more about God than it does about women? Doesn't that say that God is schizophrenic, that God made women as well as men in God's image, made women as human as men, made women as spiritual as men, and then decided that women shouldn't know it? Or worse, that women should know it but men shouldn't?

We have come to depend on the midday croissants and coffee at the "Vie De France." Most of all I like to sit in the window and watch the people, many of them in from the countrysides to "see China first." And "only," probably. I mean, where else can the Chinese go but China?

Today, as I sat at the tiny table in the little coffee bar, I noticed an old woman on a three-legged stool, a board across her knees, selling combs. "Poor woman," I thought as I got up to leave. "I'll buy her combs so she can leave this corner and go home for the rest of the day."

She was propped against the wall of the shop, hardly noticeable in the midst of the swarming crowd. I fingered every comb on the board. "How much?" I gestured and held up one finger. "Fine," I said, calculating for a moment and then picking up all the hand-carved combs in front of her. "I'll take all six." "No," she shook her head and took four of them back. I motioned at the combs again and pushed the money toward her. "No," she indicated with new vigor and a touch of annoyance. I frowned a little and looked around. What was I doing wrong? The usual Chinese crowd had gathered to watch the show. "I want to buy all six combs," I said slowly and clearly to no one in particular and everyone in general, hoping that someone in the group of younger people might be able to speak enough English to help me. The Chinese conferred among themselves. The younger people explained to her what I wanted, but the old lady got even more adamant. She had clearly understood that I wanted to buy all the combs she had. Finally, someone explained to me shyly, "There are too much women." I frowned again. "There are what?" I asked. The old lady went on scolding. "There are too much women," the younger people repeated. The old lady, exasperated with me, swept her hands across the crowds in a grand, broad demonstration of the problem. And I finally got it: If I bought all her combs, she meant, what would be left for everybody else? So, without my knowing it, she had rationed me to two combs. It was more important to her to provide for others as far as she could rather than make the profit that my sure sale promised her. I stood there a little dumbfounded for a few seconds, then, a little sheepishly, paid for two combs and moved away out of the glare of the crowd. I have a feeling that these people, formed in the fine art of family and the depth of a single culture, are not going to like capitalism at all. And I had just learned plenty myself, come to think of it.

We walked through the local market most of the afternoon, eating cold noodles with the rest of the city and being brushed aside stall after stall by bands of roving Chinese students, all holding on to one another as they went. This is not a collection of individuals. This is a people.

The Summer Palace is a breathtaking place. We got there too late to take a speedboat around the lake to the Temple of the Dragon, but I loved it and would like to come back. Someday. The next time I am in Beijing. I will remember to take a picnic and stay all day long. "The next time I am in Beijing." Ah, what a wonderful thing it is to have a sense of humor.

September 15, 1995

It is the final day of the Conference. The morning briefing was a quiet one. There was more a sense of emotional depletion in the room now than there was of exhilaration. These women had exhausted themselves. Now all they could do was wait – and hope – that the work of their lives, this Magna Carta for women, would be accepted by the assembly, would be honored by the nations. Women had worked through the night to make compromise with elements on both ends of the ideological spectrum.

Lesbians wanted sexual rights – a phrase interpreted by religious groups as the promotion of homosexuality rather than as freedom from civil discrimination – explicitly included in the document. But the gay community had been bartered off for some other dimension of women's lives. The fact that the document accepts a woman's right to control her own sexuality, some said, was a great victory and, though not explicit, did in the final analysis assure all sexual rights nevertheless. The gay community, I could see from the disappointment on some of the faces around me, doubts the fact. What was clear to them was that it was now certifiably illegal to discriminate on the basis of color, infirmity, race or gender alone, but not as clearly illegal to discriminate against homosexuals. The question seems to remain whether or not it will still be holy to put people out of jobs and homes because of a sexual orientation that hardly anyone anymore thinks is really "chosen."

Religious groups – Muslim Nations and the Holy See particularly – wanted a footnote in the Platform claiming a kind of cultural-theological caveat recognizing that anything in the document that conflicted with religious custom or law was not binding. They meant inheritance rights, divorce, legalized abortion, sexual rights and "family," as it has been traditionally defined. The footnote asserting religious belief as a right to abrogate the document had been eliminated, too, but the word was that without it these groups would accept the document only with reservation. They would promise to implement only those elements of it that did not conflict with Islamic law. I wondered what would happen to women who live in Islamic countries but are not Islamic. God, it seems, is still an excuse to control women and to eliminate them as moral agents of the human race.

NGO representatives still wanted a stronger Declaration – the cover letter that introduces the draft document – than had finally been agreed upon in the government delegations. They had, in fact, gone so far as to stay up all night and write an alternative statement to the one about to be approved by the governments of the world. No doubt about it: people were exhausted and edgy, disappointed and elated all at once.

The situation was very tense. I felt that nations who issued reservations on the basis of religious law would, in the long run, simply isolate themselves from mainstream practices and do little or no harm to the world at large. Sad as it might be for the women of those regions, at least there would be a world standard for the world community to work toward, to cherish as the ideal. The woman next to me felt very differently about the thing, however. The rest of the document, she argued, had been weakened considerably to meet fundamentalist needs. If they were going to reserve their commitments in the end, despite all the negotiation, it was her opinion that the rest of their concerns ought to have been ignored as well. She raises the essential question, of course. The UN operates on consensus. The argument for this kind of model is that, since the UN cannot mandate anything for anyone, effectiveness demands total agreement. It is an entirely new way of doing politics, a model that differs radically from the operational principles of the world around it. The model demands respect. It forces nothing but encourages and persuades nations to move in concert together, even at the most minimal of levels if necessary. As a result, however, any one nation can block passage of an entire document. Of course, the question then is whether or not UN Documents are too bland by definition to have much meaning anywhere. Maybe. But then again, it seems to me that a document that admits that women have a major human and social problem that has to be rectified if the human race is to be human has got to be better than the thousands of years of total disregard for the question that has preceded it.

World Bank president, John Wolfensohn, addressed the NGO briefing and stayed for questions before going to address the Plenary Session of the UN Conference this morning. It was an important and respectful presence. They had, for instance, made an announcement before John Wolfensohn spoke that the World Trade Organization "didn't have enough money to send anybody" to the Conference. (I made a mental note to have my ears checked when I got back to the States. Surely I misunderstood the announcement. This has got to be akin to Santa Claus saying that he didn't deliver any toys to girls on Christmas Eve because his reindeer weren't horses.)

I liked the fact that John Wolfensohn had come. I liked what he had to say. I believe he is being sincere in his recognition of the basic economic inequities in the present Structural Adjustment Programs being imposed on debtor nations. Whether the World Bank itself will respond to these needs remains the question, of course, but if not they cannot claim that it's because they never heard or did not understand. What John Wolfensohn heard from the women at this conference made clear the kind of frustration that comes when a woman begins to realize that it is powerless women who, in the long run, are the ones actually paying the debts of the men around them. It is the educational, health care, and development programs most related to the lives and needs of women that are eliminated first in nations required to cut internal expenditures in order to pay more and more of the country's GNP on debt reduction service. The World Bank calls such national budget cutbacks "Structural Adjustment Programs." The people affected by them call them SAP's. There's a message there somewhere.

The real point of the meeting is that John Wolfensohn came to the meeting at all, to meet women, to listen to them, to hold himself and the Bank accountable to them because women are organizing to demand it. Maybe men are beginning to get the idea. Women have had enough. Maybe women are beginning to get the idea, too: it is time to say "Enough" everywhere. The high point of the meeting for me was when a 23-year-old young woman from Tobago stood up, introduced herself and said, "Mr. Wolfensohn, I hear you say that you will change things at the World Bank. But I really don't care about what you promise to us today. I care about what you do for the rest of your term there. What I want is your promise to meet me the day after you finish being president so we can talk then about what changes you made in the World Bank, not now." And she walked across the front of the cavernous meeting room, stretched up to the dais on which he sat and extended her hand. "Is that a promise?" she said. And John Wolfensohn reached over the dais, took her hand in return and said quite clearly, "Young woman, that is a promise." The ballroom erupted in applause. I made a note of the incident. I will wait to see.

At 10:30 a.m., after doing a few interviews with members of the foreign press who had taken to interviewing one another since there was no other information available, I waited for Gail to get in from the hotel to meet me for breakfast. Or rather, given all the last-minute flurry in the press room and the unending string of closing questions, in the final analysis she waited for me, I guess. All I really knew was that after six weeks of having my world move under me 24 hours a day, allowing myself to sleep in for a change might have been a holier approach to life than racing to briefings and meetings at the crack of dawn. I saw her at the end of the room, looking rested and energetic after a long night and slow morning, and made a mental note to be a little less compulsive about work in the next life.

But not now. Now what is important is that we leave something that will make the life of the women who follow us free of this, free to do more than this with their lives. So what do we have to show for it all?

Platform for Action

The Beijing Platform for Action may be a hodge-podge of consensus statements, a dry and murky piece of prose, a wasteland of political innuendo, but it is at the same time a thing of beauty in its ideals and its insights. Beijing did not define problems. After 20 years of research and relentless pursuit of statistical data, anecdotal experiences, custom, and the economic realities of the women of the world, we know the problems now. Beijing took a further step than all the UN Conferences on Women before it. Beijing began the long, hard process of designing solutions.

I looked at the document that had been passed and began to realize what has been happening these past years. When the first UN Conference on Women was convened in Mexico City in 1975, we knew the number of whales in the world but we did not know the number of women. In too many areas of the world, women were not considered important enough even to count in the national census. Now, thanks to the focus brought by the United Nations then in Mexico, in 1980 in Copenhagen, and in 1985 in Nairobi, women's issues have become an international agenda item.

The Beijing document identifies 12 areas of critical concern to the lives of women, 12 areas of life that fall most severely on the backs of women: Where there is poverty, women are most poor. Women aren't hired for prestigious jobs because, we're told, "they're not equipped to handle them," but countries won't educate girls in order to get them equipped for the positions that bring the money, bring the security, bring the prestige, bring the power. Women are underfed, overworked and undeveloped in most parts of the world, used to breed the rest of the world but uncared-for themselves. Domestic violence against women, one of the major causes of female death even in the so-called "developed" world, is ignored, theologized, trivialized and largely unpunished. Women have become instruments of war, raped for the service of soldiers, displaced as a result of the wars men fight to "protect" them and sterilized to destroy the enemy. Women live in a morass of economic inequalities that starve them to death despite their contributions to the economy and their necessity to the system. Women are kept out of the decision-making arenas that then decide their fate for generations. If they are hired in the public sector, they aren't paid an equal wage for equal work, and if they're paid, they're not promoted. Women have women's rights – the rights that men decide to give them – not human rights, those qualities of human existence which no one has a right to abridge in the life of another. Women are portrayed in the media as objects for the convenience or comfort of men, helpmates and handmaidens, seldom as equals, never as superiors. Women become the powerless victims of the mismanagement of environmental resources around them. Female infanticide and the trafficking of girl-children plague women from infancy. It is a deplorable state, this degradation of the female for female's sake. It is called "civilization" and God's will. It is invisible, taken for granted, rationalized and wrong.

But men suffer, too, people say. Suffering doesn't just happen to women. And that is, indeed, true. There is a major difference in the two conditions, however. Men suffer either because the system has failed them or they have failed the system. Men do not suffer simply because they were born male. Women, on the other hand, live lesser lives at every level of society simply because they are women. Worse, women suffer because men somewhere have decided that dependence, violence, servitude, ignorance, deprivation and powerlessness is a woman's role. Someplace men wrote it down: in a biology book, in a philosophy book, in a theology book. And then they wrote their books into law. And then they wrote their laws into life. For a woman, they say deprivation is her lot in life. But they have never in their lives been more mistaken, and women have come to Beijing by the thousands to say so.

The Beijing Platform for Action has 12 sections. Each of them carries the seed of a new world for women.

1. Poverty

There are more than a billion poor people in the world today, about one-fourth of the population of the globe, who do not know where the next meal is coming from, who have no furniture in their houses, who have no houses at all, in fact. Seventy percent of them are women, and their numbers are increasing by the year. These poor women live in cardboard lean-to shacks against the back wall of the world's local Holiday Inns or on stilt houses that teeter over a riverbed. Their children defecate in city streams and sleep on mud floors. They live out of garbage cans and junk piles. And the women are helpless to do a thing about it. They don't have the education it would take to get a job, even if there were any available. They have no property rights so they can't buy land, even if they have the money to do so. And without land as collateral, they can't borrow money either. They can't even inherit money because women, their cultures and religious traditions say, are taken care of by men and so don't need it. I remembered the stories told by missionaries about the situations of widows in parts of Africa and the Middle East, many of whom are moved out of their homes before the husband's burial ceremony is even over. I have seen pictures of widows wailing at the funerals of their husbands. Now I began to realize that they may well have been crying as much for the fact that they themselves were left alive in such conditions – poor, displaced and useless – as for the fact that he was now dead. A woman's place is in the home, men preach, and then when the man dies, they take her out of it because it doesn't belong to her.

By the end of the 1980s, approximately 75% of all poverty in the US was concentrated among women, particularly single mothers and older African-American women. Their income, researchers tell us, is 23% below the poverty line. They live in my block and eat at our soup kitchen. They are decent women left to fend for themselves in a society that resents charity and will not do justice to women. So their lives deteriorate to the level of the subsistence society around them.

The Beijing Document insists that governments analyze the effect of present economic policies on women, that they evaluate the effectiveness of anti-poverty programs and that they provide access to resources – to credit, property rights and social security – so that women can develop the economic independence that men take for granted. If all the property is in his name, if there is no way that a woman can get the collateral she needs to begin a small business, let alone to build a house, if the social programs that pertain most to women and children are the first to go when the men of a country finally curb their excesses by austerity programs borne by women, then we must face the fact that the lives of men are feathered at the expense of the lives of women. The role of a man is to provide for his family, they tell us with evangelical fervor. They neglect to say how a woman will provide for them when the men do not.

I thought of Mkambi and Gloria, Nancy and Aura, women I know who are on their own now. They stand in my mind here in Beijing as a sign of all the women of the world, some of them widowed, some abandoned, some the products of bad divorces, some the victims of romantic notions of marriages guaranteed to make them happy ever after, but which simply left them poor and with children or, worse, poor and alone. I couldn't help but wonder what would happen if the senators and representatives from Pennsylvania who were busy cutting welfare programs would ever talk to one of them, sit in their kitchens, or live for a month on the money these women make at part-time jobs.

What do all of those things demand of the rest of us, of me, I wondered? What does it say about elections and campaign promises and the movement away from social compassion to social cruelty in the United States?

One thing I knew, these women friends of mine needed the Beijing Platform for Action badly.

2. Education and Training

Almost two-thirds of all the illiterate of the world are women and girls. They are denied schooling in some places, taken out of school early in others. In rural areas, illiteracy rates for women are often two to three times the illiteracy rate of women in urban areas. Even in countries where women routinely receive higher education, whole categories of professions are closed to them. They are left to earn their living with few premium services to offer, few employable skills to barter for bread, whatever their brainpower. And why? "If women are as intelligent as men," I heard a Middle Eastern ruler say to an interviewer once, "where are their musicians, their artists? Such talents do not require education." I felt myself bristle. Women's paintings are in basements and attics, unvalued and unhung by the male curators of the world. Even the history of women in the art world has been lost, just as their talent was lost to it as well. I wondered as I listened to him how many people realized that women were kept out of art schools and, as a result, away from the patrons they would need to cultivate their talent. European moralists taught that women should be barred from the very centers that developed the Michelangelos and Bocaccios of the culture on the grounds that for a women to paint nudes – one of the required courses in medieval art institutes – was unseemly, was heinous. Women musicians were not hired on the grounds that they were not strong enough for the rigors of playing the violin in orchestras that performed night after night, though the same women could be up night after night caring for children. Women actresses were kept off the stage because drama ranked as a lewd occupation. So men played women's parts and bore no moral opprobrium for it. The first woman doctor in New York City was driven from her office in the early 20th century by the men of the city on the grounds that it was "immoral" for a woman to be a doctor. Women found themselves excluded everywhere because what men said was moral for men, they also said was immoral for women.

Generation after generation have cut women out of the very arenas that would have given them economic security, confirmed their intellectual contributions to humankind, made them adult participants in an adult world.

I had been a high-school teacher once. In my own lifetime, I had seen the smartest students in the school, girls, denied access to the best colleges in the country, the best departments in the universities, the best-paying professions in society on the grounds that women did not go to such places, do such things, need such money. I saw the headmaster of a school arbitrarily reverse the order of awardees to the National Honor Society, ranking the lower-scoring boys above the three highest-standing girls, regardless of their grade point averages. He rested his argument on the grounds that the boys of the school "lacked role models" and they were the ones who "really needed to go to college." What's more, he saw no injustice in this treatment of the girls. No, I said to myself as I thought about the document that was about to be endorsed by the nations of the world, no need to go to Ethiopia to find discrimination. We had a long history of it right here in that so-called bastion of feminism, the United States of America.

Yet the education of women affects the quality of family life as do few other things in society. It takes an educated woman to maintain a quality home. It takes an educated woman to raise healthy, well-nourished children. It takes an educated woman to raise the educational level of the entire family. It takes an educated woman to be an agent of social change.

Yet, in whole regions of the world even today, girls receive little or no education at any level, let alone access to higher education. Girls are married off early, children come early, death comes early. And where schools do exist for both boys and girls, gender-based roles and sex-stereotypes continue to be used, continue to be taught, trapping bright girls in the second-class positions that maintain society as men like it, but bring little or no personal rewards, little or no sense of personal achievement or social significance, little or no economic security for women. Girls have minds they are not permitted to use in a society becoming more technological, more science-oriented by the day.

The Platform for Action sets the year 2005 as the target date for closing the gender gap in primary and secondary school education, including for pregnant girls, and the year 2015 as the year by which universal primary education ought to be achieved throughout the world. Governments promised to reduce the female illiteracy rate by one-half by the year 2000 and provide women the retraining needed to enable them to enter the labor market in a changing society. How is it, I wondered, that the human race had ever gotten to the point where we could put a man on the moon and leave 60 million women unable to sign their names and never see the disparity between the two goals? How can we ever have women in decision-making roles who cannot even read the problem before them, let alone bring to bear on it the best information of the time? What kind of throw-away rag dolls had we made of women anyway? Who had done this thing? What would God think?

3. Health

The average life expectancy is 79 years for a woman in Western Europe, North America, Australia and New Zealand. This figure for Sub-Saharan Africa is 54. Why? Because women die from being women, that's why. A woman's risk of dying in childbirth is 1 in 25-40 in developing countries, as compared to 1 in 3000 in developed countries.

It isn't what a woman needs that determines what she gets. It is class and culture that determine a woman's access to health services. In India, girls are four times more likely than boys to suffer from the anemia that comes from undernourishment or pregnancy, and 40 times less likely than boys to be taken to a doctor. Every year, over half-a-million women die from complications due to pregnancy in areas where obstetricians are at a premium, if they exist at all, and prenatal care a myth.

Women in developing countries are fed less than men, cared for less than men, turned as children into sexually active women before their bodies can bear it. Girl-children become the property of men who beat them, maltreat them and abandon them at their whim and fancy. Women, the UN bulletins tell us, "now constitute 40% of the HIV-infected adults." By the year 2000, researchers say, more than 15 million women – most of them faithful consorts of unfaithful partners or captive companions to unscrupulous traffickers – stand to be infected with the virus, of whom about four million may die. For these young girls, there is no recourse to health systems or to social service centers. They are forced into street-corner prostitution, lured out of villages into brothels in the pursuit of decent jobs, married off to men who take multiple sex partners for granted and bring the virus home to faithful wives, or used and abused in the forced labor systems in which they find themselves in the process of fleeing from one slavery to another,

New York City, newspapers report, is full of sweatshops. Young women brought to the United States under the pretext of advancement find themselves left to "pay off their passage" to trafficking rings in illegal industries, in slave labor conditions, for indefinite periods of time.

Women live marginated lives and bear the mental stress of that. Women live longer than men in the Western world and bear the economic strain of that. And, in some parts of the world, women live over-medicated lives designed to dull but not to lift the burdens that cause their pain in the first place.

I thought of Zelda, mentally ill and "de-institutionalized," who in the richest country of the world simply slipped through the cracks. She lived with us for awhile, and then disappeared one day, just sane enough to go, just sick enough to be unable to come back. She wandered the streets of Erie, Pennsylvania, raving but harmless, raped and robbed repeatedly, left in city parks to die, or doomed to float through life on a bus between Tampa and Buffalo. We looked for her and lost her among the nameless hordes of women in this world who exist unseen by the male legislators of the world, too poor to care about, too useless to matter.

The document says that women must be given reproductive rights and health care, the one almost invariably linked to the other in a woman's life. The question is not how many children a woman may have; the question is how many children a woman wants. The document says that "the human rights of women include their right to have control over and decide freely and responsibly on matters related to their sexuality, including sexual and reproductive health, free of coercion, discrimination and violence." Tell that, I thought, to the 5000 women a day who suffer genital mutilation so that the men of the culture can have the satisfaction of knowing that the "property" they get at marriage is both good goods and rendered domestically stable by the surgical control of their sexual responses. After all, why would they stray? There is no pleasure for them in marriage, this one or any other, now. Tell that to the women being forcibly sterilized as a kind of ethnic cleansing. Tell that to the men who impregnate women whose bodies cannot carry another child.

To those women, the Beijing document means life.

4. Violence Against Women

Women are an endangered species. It was the sheer volume of material on violence about women that made me begin to wonder about the mental health, the intelligence, the humanity of men. And I didn't like the feelings. I know good men, kind men, men who tread lightly upon the earth, who go through life with a poet's pain for the world, who do no harm to anything, let alone to a woman. How was it, then, that men as a class could abuse women the way they do? How is it that other men can allow it? What is it that gives men the unedited notion that women are theirs to do with as they like? It was the first thing my mother taught me and I remember it well, "Men think that they own women," she said. "Make sure that you can take care of yourself, Joan." The proof of the position is appalling: In India, five women are burned in dowry-related deaths every day. If a husband is unsatisfied with the size of the dowry he gets with one wife, he douses her with gasoline, burns her to death and marries someone else for a second dowry. In Papua New Guinea, 67% of the women suffered domestic violence. In the United States, a woman is physically abused every eight seconds, and one is raped every six minutes, the government says, and study after study confirms it. Cultures call it "manliness" and say that "boys will be boys." How can this possibly be?

But beatings are not the only kind of violence that women suffer. Women for whom jobs are scarce to begin with, lower paying always, and most vulnerable in times of downsizing, live knowing that at any moment they may be expected to keep the few jobs they get by paying sexual favors for them. Women become the commodities of the world, passed from man to man for his use, his advancement, his comfort, his convenience. Nor is it confined to class. Intelligent women, young women, professional women, all women know that they are in danger at all times. And when will violence against women end? Only when it becomes a felony and not a "mistake," or a social assumption or a "domestic problem." It will end only when society, good men and courageous women, demands that it ends.

The Beijing Document requires that governments provide shelters for battered women, punishment for perpetrators, research and therapy to curb that kind of disorder, and strict penalties for sexual harassment.

Journalists covering the O.J. Simpson trial reported that men spend an average of four years in jail for wife-killing. More than any thermometer, data like that measures the extent of the illness in this society – and why it continues. "I just don't know why a man like Warren Moon would be labeled over and over again as a 'wife-beater,' " the man said. "It only happened once and now they never forget it." I wondered if he would have said the same thing about a man who embezzled his bank only once, or the man who was an arsonist only once, or the man who knifed his boss only once? I said a prayer of thanks for Beijing and the women for whom this document was really a Platform for Action.

5. Armed Conflict

No one suffers from war as much as women and children, who do not start it, do not fight it and do not want it. No one. A conference fact sheet reported that, at the beginning of this century, about 90% of the casualties of war were military. Now, the report went on, about 90% of the casualties of war are civilian. I have been part of the peace movement for 25 years, but no one told me that. No one told me that the men of the world are now really waging war on the women of this world. But I should have known. After all, the atomic bombing of Hiroshima was the first time in recorded history that wholesale carnage of civilians was justified on the grounds that "it saved soldiers."

Robert McNamara and the General Vo Nguyen Jiap, who was responsible for the defeat of the US Armed Forces in Vietnam, agreed on television recently that the war had been a "mistake." I wondered as I listened to the report whether or not the women burned out of villages, the children who were napalmed, the girls who were raped were so easily able to write the whole thing off as "a mistake." I wondered how it was that those two men could say such a thing now and be called "experts," but that those who said it in the 60s were called traitors.

How is it that men have to be told, shown, convinced that sexual intimidation, the barbarism of war, the wholesale use of force in a species whose glory lies in its trumpeted rationality is wild, insane violence to begin with? Is it testosterone poisoning? Is it hormonal imbalance? Do they all need more estrogen in their systems to be able to act like human beings? It's a thought. The minute a woman so much as cries, they give her a pill, a psychiatrist, a doctor or a marriage counselor. They label the syndrome and set out to cure the problem. But when men go on a rampage through the streets, they don't call it sickness. They call it war and bring out a bishop or two to bless their bombs. They say the violence is patriotic and brave and honorable and all good things. There has to be something wrong with that.

As a result, women and their dependents constitute 75% of the world's 23 million refugees. Rape has become an instrument of war. In recent years, the United Nations has documented mass rape in Cambodia, Liberia, Peru, Somalia and Uganda. In Kigali, between April 1994 and April 1995, UN documents say, 15,700 women and girls aged 13-65 were raped, more than 1,100 gave birth and 5,200 had abortions. As a Catholic, I couldn't help but wonder who the church considered excommunicated in that situation: the women who had the abortions or the men who forcibly impregnated them. One act they tell me is natural, the other one they tell me with the same authority is absolutely immoral. I admit it: that kind of skewed morality is oftentimes lost on me. More than 20,000 women were reported to have been raped in Bosnia and Herzegovina in the first months of the war. They were herded into rape hotels, then murdered by the men who used them, or abandoned by the men to whom they were returned, many of them bearing the enemy's children. All of them considered unclean, dishonorable, ignominious. All of them bearing the burden of the sins of the men around them.

Women walk the roads away from the homes the men of the country destroyed in order to "protect." Women live in the refugee camps where they are unsafe. They find themselves in strange countries where they are unprotected, unsupported, unwelcome and unqualified for care. They find themselves at the mercy of a world that does not even know they exist.

The Beijing Platform for Action calls for protection for refugees, programs to enable them to function, to work, to live in new environments, safe passage through war zones and counseling in situations of trauma, torture and violence.

I saw before me, as I held the document, all their faces in all the newspapers of the world – women crushed, staring, bleeding, numbed, shocked and empty. Fleeting faces in pain, never seen again, never thought about again, never sung about in war songs, never decorated, never glorified – the women of the wars of the world, the uncounted victims and their smothered screams.

6. Economic Participation

Women are the primary producers of the food of the world. Women are the backbone of every society. Women maintain the domestic systems that enable all the major economic systems of the world. But they make few, if any, of the business decisions of society. They themselves lack equal access to the means of production. They are denied capital, credit, technology and input into the economic superstructures of every society on earth. Even the work they do themselves is unpaid, underpaid and undervalued. Men do the "important" things like go to meetings and make decisions. Women do the "other" things – the things that make society run and decisions work, like cook the meals, wash the clothes, send all the notices, organize all the work forces, provide all the support services that produce and process the products. Just look around and see who serves the food at McDonald's and clerks in every department store and answers phones in every law office and puts books together in every mailing house and, everywhere, takes good meetings from the agenda stage to the delivery stage.

About 32%, 900 million people, of the global labor force are women, most of them relegated to the production end of the job, to the lowest level of its pay scale, not to its management. Less than 4% of the economic ministers of the world are women. Clearly, we take women's labor but we don't want their experience, their opinions, or their ideas on the subject. Women work; men decide the hows and whats and whys and whens of it all. In the 1000 largest corporations outside the United States, only one in 100 executives is a woman. In this country, too, where women have been a factor in the labor force for well over half a century, female managers – the 8 out of every 100 there are – are still concentrated at lowest levels of the organization. We can hardly call the situation "accidental."

Worst of all, female wage scales cry to heaven for vengeance. Women are paid barely two-thirds of what men make for the same work, despite the fact that bread and heat and light and rent cost a woman and her family exactly what they cost a man and his. We pay men "a living wage" and women "pin money." The word for that is "exploitation."

We hire women part-time, give them no benefits and blame it all on pregnancy. We have made child-bearing a disease and called it "motherhood." We have made "fathering" a child an event and "mothering" a child a lifetime definition.

The fact is that industry is organized around men. Companies provide plenty of parking lots and golf courses, but not enough day care centers. They give bonuses but not flex-time. They will hire one man to do one job, but not a man and a woman to do the same job at a single wage so that both of them can raise their child together. They will pay for business lunches but not for family sick care time.

We talk about the "family" and organize life around the corporation. Churches preach about motherhood but miss the concept of parenting completely. In most countries, women work approximately twice the unpaid time men do, UN reports confirm, except for Japan where women do nine times more unpaid work than men do.

The Platform for Action calls for the end of economic discrimination, for equal pay for equal work, and the valuation of women's unremunerated work. Women are not charity cases. Their work in the home is the foundation of the entire system. They deserve every single program they get. Argentina, for instance, has calculated the value of domestic activity carried on by Argentinean women and estimate that it amounts to between 28-49% of its

GNP! If women's work in the home, all 9 trillion dollars worth of it, is as valuable as men say it is, is as necessary to the system as economists say it is, is as dignified an occupation as churches say it is, then why isn't it counted in the GNP? Why isn't it counted on the tax forms? Why isn't it counted anywhere?

The Beijing Platform for Action charges nations with the responsibility to end discrimination based on sex, to equalize wages, to see that women get access to capital and credit, to create satellite national accounts that record the value of women's unpaid domestic work, to bring women into the decision-making arena of the economic order. It demands an end to economic discrimination based on gender. It rejects the feminization of poverty.

It is a document long in coming, late in coming, but written in every woman's heart.

7. *Women in Power*

Only 10 of the governments of the world were headed by women in 1994. Twenty-five countries, half of them in Asia and the Pacific, had no women at either the ministerial or sub-ministerial level. Only 10% of the members of legislative bodies of the world – and even fewer of the appointed ministerial positions in national governments – are held by women, though in Scandinavian countries about one-third of the ministers are women, and in Sweden women have parity with men in ministerial posts. In every other country, the figures are painfully low, even in nations where the women's movement has been a visible force for years. The high cost of seeking office, the limited resources of women supporters, the almost unshared responsibilities of homemaking – all keep women from even seeking office. They don't have the money to run for office, they don't have the time to run for office, they don't have the support personnel they need to be able to run for office. "The only thing that an intelligent woman lacks that the average man has," the wag says, "is a good wife." Like him, she needs someone to do the cooking while she runs the campaign. She needs wealthy patrons, men who do not give their political campaign money to men only. And she needs a good staff, people who will work for a women, under a woman, with a woman. Without those things the grueling work of running for offices long under the control of male networks, even in the most democratic countries in the world, looms almost impossible. As a result, society is deprived of a feminine perspective, a feminine value system and a feminine voice. But until that happens, who will even know what a woman's experience of life is, let alone legislate for it?

More than 100 countries of the world have no women in parliament at all. Even at the United Nations itself, only six of the 185 member countries have women permanent representatives. Yet, where women are in government, the record is clear. They vote differently from men, they have different priorities, different concerns, different solutions to social problems than men do. Men do not speak for women. The needs of the whole world are not being met by parliaments as they are presently constructed. Until women have access to elected offices, even democracies will simply be masking another kind of dictatorship – the imposition of male agendas over female ones.

The Beijing Platform for Action moves governments to require gender analysis from every aspect of government. It mandates the United Nations itself to put women into senior positions. It asks governments themselves to model the presence of women at the highest levels, to hear their voices, to solicit their input, to honor their agendas. Until we see women in positions of decision-making, we will never put them there.

8. Mechanisms for Advancement

The absence of women in government presents one problem to society. The absence of women from the public arena in general presents an equally serious gap in the human condition. Women are seldom recognized as leaders in almost any public arena, sometimes for the same reasons that women are lacking in the political system – time and money – but sometimes because the images of women provided by male psychologists and theologians render them passive, docile, servile, fearful and basically incapable of providing insight, inspiration and organization. Churches have long taught the "headship" of men, all biblical figures of women leaders – Deborah, Judith, Mary Magdalene – to the contrary. But equality in decision-making is basic to any hope for equality anywhere.

When I read the document's call for women in public positions, I thought of the schools where the majority of teachers are women but the principal is a man. I remembered all of the theology faculties in the church world that teach about God and ethics and history only from a male point of view. I thought of the sisters who taught us catechism every day of our lives and then were obstructed from preaching that same Gospel from a pulpit. I thought of all the supermarkets where I had ever grocery-shopped that had rows of long-term female checkout clerks and one 22-year-old male manager. I knew that women would never be thought of as leaders by these people as long as these situations stayed this way.

The Beijing document calls for gender balance on commissions, committees, public platforms, private boards and institutional planning programs. It asks for statistical analysis so that we can all come to see the unseen, the absence of women from the centers of life. It asks governments to integrate women in decision-making in all departments and all levels. It asks for mentoring programs for women, for courses in self-esteem, for mechanisms designed specifically to nominate women for positions in the United Nations itself. I remembered John Wolfensohn saying that he had created a board in the World Bank, the purpose of which was to evaluate all programming from a woman's perspective and report directly to him. I wondered how long it would be before many other institutions in the world would do the same – like the local banks, the local newspapers, the local community foundations, the local unions, the local civic systems. And the minute I thought about it, I knew that life as we know it would change drastically if that ever happened.

I realized how badly women needed the Beijing Platform for Action if the world was ever to be whole.

9. Human Rights

"A right," past Attorney General Ramsey Clarke said, "is not something than anyone can give you. A right is something that no one can take away." Men cannot "give" women their human rights. They can only agree not to take them away. Those rights go with being human. They are inalienable, inherent, unarguable. Now. But not always. Not for everyone. This white Western world never really recognized the concept of universal human rights for centuries. And even after the Enlightenment, there were still questions about Indians, about blacks, about women. The first questions contested their full humanity. Only later, only now, are some peoples even beginning to ask about the rights that the mere fact of being human implies for women as well as for men. Until a 1989 legal reform, for instance, a husband in Ecuador had the right to force his wife to live with him, no matter how abusive he may have been. Laws in Chile and Guatemala specifically exonerate a man who agrees to marry the girl he has raped because he has restored the honor of her family. In the secular laws of a number of countries, only a husband, not the wife, can obtain a divorce on the grounds of adultery.

It's 1995 and we still need to argue the point for women. We still need documents asserting the situation for women. That ought to tell us something about the way the world goes together. That ought to say something to people who still "Tsk, tsk" over the Women's Movement. The Women's Movement is not asking for the destruction of men; it's asking for the human recognition of women – for the full recognition of women as humans!

This document says that "Every person should be entitled to participate in, contribute to and enjoy cultural, economic, political and social development." Where women are concerned, the statement is almost laughable. Women without education, without economic security, without participation in the public arena and without scope for full development do not have human rights. That includes most of the women of the world. Most of them. Yet. Now. And where the laws exist, the practices do not because the women either do not know about the laws or they have no power to enforce them, no one to protect them, no way to promote them.

To the very night of the passage of this document, only 139 of the 185 member countries of the United Nations have accepted the "Convention on the Elimination of All Forms of Discrimination against Women." What we have when women are treated well, then, is benignity, not justice. What we have when women are treated poorly is simply the latest rendering of what men say that women deserve.

The Beijing Platform for Action requires the United Nations itself to provide the research, assessments, education and public information it will take to unmask the inhumanity suffered by women from womb to tomb simply because they are women. We need institutions to watchdog the world's way with women. We need women in the court and penal system to watchdog it themselves.

We need to "ensure equality and non-discrimination under the law," the document says. I thought of all the women of the world who didn't even know that laws on their behalf exist because they aren't written in their language or they have never been allowed to learn to read their language. I couldn't help but think of the difference in length of prison terms. In the United States itself, men serve shorter sentences for violent crimes than women do for lesser criminal offenses. I thought of the women who have had husbands arrested for battering, only to see them released the next morning with a smile and a handslap. I thought of the fathers who went free despite incest charges. I thought of women who worked for years in businesses that never promoted them, never gave them incremental salary increases, never provided benefits and never permitted them to join a union. I thought of all the little girls of the world who were denied education, inheritance rights, contract opportunities, sexual autonomy and representation because they were girls. I thought of women abandoned, abused, made poor and ignored because they were women.

Do we still need the Beijing Platform for Action? NO, we need it more than ever.

10. Mass Media

We live up to our images of ourselves. And we live down to them, as well. As little boys, men stretch to the stature of their heroes. Women don't have to stretch at all. On the contrary, whatever great plans they would like to make for their lives, they learn early to shrink to the size of the cloth that has been prepared for them: helper, aide, assistant, server. Never inventor, thinker, tycoon, genius, leader,

The role of the media in the social status and recognition of women cannot be exaggerated. What we see around us is what we believe reality to be. The options presented are the options we choose from to design for ourselves. Women's reality, the media suggests, is frilly and female to the point of the extreme, a sexual experience more than an intellectual companion, the creature who dresses up in exotic dresses and short skirts to flip the cards on the game show, not the man who asks the questions.

Why? Because men's perception of what women should be gluts the airwaves. Men control the media, men direct the media, men write and produce the shows and men reflect in the media, therefore, what their own ideas of reality, of the roles and nature of women are or ought to be. The stereotypes – limited, superficial, and negative – go on being reproduced, year after year after year. The Public Broadcasting System shows a vignette of Eleanor Roosevelt or Florence Nightingale or Elizabeth Cady Stanton, and the major networks show hours of prime time floozies, victims and Barbie dolls – sexy, lame-brained, and beaten.

According to the United Nations, women constitute only 25% of the personnel in both the broadcasting and the press offices of Africa, Asia and Latin America. Even in Europe, where media is more developed and audiences are more universal, only 30% of the press are women and only 36% of broadcast journalists are women. Clearly, few top positions in either area belong to women. Studies by UNESCO of 200 media organizations in 30 countries worldwide show that only seven are headed by women. A 10-country study shows that only 1.4% of TV news items deal with women's issues, and three quarters of them are presented by men. Everywhere on earth women are seen, interpreted, defined and presented through men's eyes.

Women appear in violent, degrading and pornographic productions. Traditional roles din themselves into the minds of the young – girls as well as boys. Consumerism defines them as targets and uses them as subliminal attractions to call attention to products, things that come with the car, the suit and the whiskey.

The Beijing Platform for Action sets out to shatter the process of producing women for male consumption rather than presenting women as full human beings. The document summons countries to include more women in decision-making roles in media and communication technologies, to increase the number of programs for and about women so that women's concerns can be properly addressed; to promote balanced and diverse portrayals of women; to use the media to provide training programs for women and to establish media-watch groups to monitor programming and critique its content on behalf of women.

I couldn't help but wonder what the world would look like now, what women would be doing now, if in an earlier age Eleanor Roosevelt had been as often portrayed as FDR had been, if Madame Curie had been as much a role model for girls as Dr. Salk had been for boys, if Anne Morrow Lindbergh's writings had been as advertised as Thoreau's. It is not a question to be taken lightly. Aspiration is the seed of life.

11. Environment and Development

Everywhere in the world the poor flood into urban areas, looking for the work and the food that barren areas no longer afford, that lost markets no longer provide, that agribusiness now usurps, that polluted areas now destroy. Almost one-half of the population of the world now lives in cities – taxing housing conditions, adding to garbage disposal problems, draining resources, burdening social services, creating traffic pollution, opening sores of poverty on city streets. And most of them are women and children.

Out in the countryside, the poverty is even worse. Women walk for hours down rock slopes to sell stunted fruits at far-away markets, walk miles up muddy clay paths to carry water from dry wells, live on dry diets, and die from the malnutrition that comes from the custom of feeding the men of the family first and carrying too many babies too soon and too often. But when Western help does finally come, it comes to men for men's needs. The World Bank loans go to men, the farm equipment that comes in foreign aid packages goes only to men, the agricultural training courses are given to men. Other needs are ignored or put on hold for their completion. The roads wait, the water pipes wait, the needs of the women of the area wait. Subsistence farming is done the hard way – by women. The men go into the cities to get daywork, and the salaries that go with it, while the women work to eke out an existence where no water flows, no trees grow, no fish live, no fuel is left and pollution poisons the environment. The women become scavengers, paupers on the land, forgotten, untrained and unnoticed. They cook with wood and straw and dung in poorly ventilated huts for an average of five hours a day, and live and die with respiratory infections as a result. And no one does a thing about it. On the contrary, they cut down the forests and pollute the waters and radiate the lands. It is the silent sin of the modern world. Silent because men have long been deaf to the cries of women.

What women know about farming nobody asks them. What women need for farming, nobody gives them. In Africa women do 30% of the plowing, 50% of the planting, 50% of the livestock care, 60% of the harvesting, 70% of the weeding, 85% of the processing of foodstuffs and 95% of the domestic work. And they do it without education, without resources, without professional support, without control of the functions of the market and without participation in the decision-making bodies that regulate the agricultural industries of the region. They do it on their own. They do it in the face of so-called "development" projects that have ruined the land and raped the futures of their children for the sake of commercial profiteering. And no one notices. They are, after all, only women.

Conservation, environmental management, land use and agricultural planning depend on them, but they are seldom trained for it and almost never included in the arenas where decisions are made and global interests are mediated. Yet, clearly, development programs that do not include women cannot possibly succeed.

The Platform for Action urges countries to make environmental information and education, technology and economics, science and resources available to women. It also charges nations to solicit, respect and preserve the knowledge of indigenous women about traditional medicines, as well as to share the benefits and profits that accrue to them. Traditional knowledge is not useless knowledge. We have had a good many modern "wonder-drugs" that did not work, and just as many traditional herbs and seeds and compounds that now fill health-food store shelves. It directs countries to involve women as scientists, planners and environmental engineers everywhere, so that opportunities open in this field for the development of skills that have been the work of women in large sections of the world for generation upon generation, for people after people, for culture upon culture.

The question, of course, is whether or not women can stop men from driving the world pell-mell to its own destruction. Have profit motives finally come to the point of no return? Or have they simply brought the world to the point of no return? One of those ubiquitous T-shirt sayings crossed my mind: "Listen to women. For a change," it says. But would they? Soon enough? Ever?

12. The Girl-Child

The statistics shake the soul. In 1993, 130 million children had no access to primary school; 81 million of them were girls. An estimated 450 million women in developing countries live crippled, stunted lives due to childhood protein-energy malnutrition that comes from feeding girls the leftovers of men's meals. More than 2 million girls undergo genital mutilation each year. They are married young, sold young, passed from man to man young, put to work young, and die young – if they are allowed to live at all. What Third World mother wants to bring a girl-child into the world to suffer as she has, to be rejected as she has been rejected, to be deprived of her own young life in order to breed other young lives, as she has been deprived? It is a storm of sorrow, a deluge of pain that describes the lives of the women of the world. It starts when they are infants and it follows them to their graves. Not all women find themselves in abusive situations certainly. Some of them are given to men who are very kind, very caring. Those are the lucky ones, of course. But they are given, nevertheless. They do not lead autonomous lives. They do not make decisions about schools or careers. They do not dream dreams and develop ideas. They do not travel around the world. They do not travel to the next village. They do not leave the house. They do not leave the harem. They were born to be used, abused and abandoned when no longer useful. And no one asks them what they want or what they think, ever.

I thought of the indigenous women who met in the tiny little room at the far end of the Conference Center. I wondered if they would see any change for the women of their tribes in their own lifetimes. They have lived deprived lives for generations now.

Interesting, isn't it, how no one ever accepts deprivation, they simply get accustomed to it?

The women in Beijing fashioned an international document that called for the universal protection of their daughters. They want international laws that put an end to child-marriage, to child labor, to child sexual exploitation, to trafficking in girl-children, to black-market sales of human organs gained by the kidnap, sale and murder of girls.

They want their daughters to be educated. They want their mothers to be taken care of properly. They want their sisters to become the architects of their own lives. They are not talking about hatred of men. They are talking about respect for women. They want marriages built on friendship, not servitude. They want their daughter's life to be as valuable, as valued, as their son's. They want their daughter's to be able to control their own sexuality, not to have them made captive by it. They want them to have the right to be children before they are made to be mothers.

The Platform for Action calls the nations of the world to unmask the condition of girls, of women, everywhere, to face the degradation, to repent the wrong, to repair the brokenness that exists in a world where some humans are considered more human than other humans, where some of us are considered to exist for the pleasure and the profit of the rest of us. Beijing calls us to put the world together right.

That demands a change in negative attitudes toward women. That means that all doors – all doors – must open to women. That means that the minds of women can no longer be squandered on the trivial when the problems of the world are so complex, the bodies of women can no longer abused and the lives of women can no longer be circumscribed by traditions, customs and practices that made creation a mockery, religion a sin and humanity inhuman.

The document about to be passed by the General Assembly called for new attitudes toward women, for new life for women, for a new world for both men and women alike. "Will everyone do it?" I asked myself. And I knew the answer: Not now. Not immediately, perhaps. But every minute that they delay, the court of human opinion will judge them more and more culpable, more and more reprehensible. "Social science affirms that a woman's place in society marks the level of civilization," the 19th-century American suffragist Elizabeth Cady Stanton wrote. The verdict is now for all the world to see.

We walked over to the United States Information Service Office on the second floor of the Continental Grand Hotel to pick up a copy of the Ferraro interview tape, and stopped for lunch at the restaurant there. It's time to start celebrating life a little after long weeks of arm-wrestling it. Unfortunately, I haven't recognized a thing I've eaten for so long that I don't have a clue whether it was a good meal or not. All I know is that it was not ice cream and cake, but I liked it.

The next order of the day was to stand in line, as usual, to get a ticket to the closing plenary session of the assembly. Correction: to try to get a ticket to the plenary. Ever since the first day of the Conference, the ticketing process here has been designed to create chaos and frustration. Reporters are required to stand in long lines for hours to get one of the limited number of passes to the Observer's Gallery. People who have come across the world to cover this event only to find themselves locked out of almost everything do not view the system kindly. There is no order, no central communication unit, no common set of announcements or directives to go by here. Everything runs by rumor, by word of mouth, by guess and by golly. Reporters have spent more time trying to find the story than to write the story. It is an octopus named "politics," and God only knows which tentacle will be working when, which arm we should be reaching for to shake its hand. No wonder newspapers make news instead of reporting it. The world seems intent on not giving them any.

The Plenary Session of the Conference was sheer protocol. Everything had, of course, been sewed up in best negotiating style before the delegates walked onto the floor. It was simply a matter now of sitting through the four long hours where protocol violated reason. And yet, there was an excitement in the gallery. You could feel it all around you. Observers broke into applause as nation after nation endorsed the document.

We left the assembly after the reading of the reservations. The Vatican had very deftly decided against specifying their remaining objections aloud – "in the spirit of consensus" – and left it to the Muslim fundamentalists to take the international spotlight for their objections to an expanded definition of family, the call for equal inheritance rights for girl-children, the decriminalization of abortion and "anything else contrary to Islamic religious law."

It is a major question, this use of religion to keep women under the control of men, and men the dominant members of the society. Can governments contravene such things? Should they? Where do theocratic states and human rights conflict? Or do they?

It was a warm and lovely night in Beijing. We sat and talked for hours. Had anything happened here? Was this simply cruel ritual – the kind that raises hopes and then dashes them against a stone – or was it the beginning of a new world for women? Would anybody listen? On the one hand, was it worthwhile to have come to Beijing? On the other hand, would you have missed it for the world? And what really counts: the document that was just passed here or the women who met here? By midnight I almost felt normal again. Maybe the real value of the Conference lay in neither the document nor the networking. Maybe it was simply the matter of the Conference itself, the legitimizing of the question, the focus on the issues, that made the real impact. I for one had never read in full all the documents that came out of Mexico City or Copenhagen or Nairobi. I simply knew that women had gone there on my behalf, and that having found one another, we would never, ever be alone again.

Fourth UN Conference on Women, Part I

The Fourth UN Conference on Women in Beijing has turned a corner in responding to the conditions of women around the world. But it has not been an easy corner to turn. The longer I'm in Beijing, the more my respect is growing for the biblical story of the Tower of Babel. I think I'm also beginning to understand a little better now what destroyed it. In Babel "the language was confused." Everyone shouted to be heard in a language that no one else could comprehend. At the half-way point of the Fourth UN Conference on Women, women from around the world are clamoring for action from their governments, but the clamoring takes a variety of accents.

Coming to an understanding among the governments of the world about the kinds of programs needed to improve the living conditions of the women of the world makes Beijing a far more volatile place than were the three UN Women's Conferences that preceded it. It is one thing for groups to agree on principles for action, as the governments of the world did at the women's conferences in Mexico City, Copenhagen and Nairobi. It is another thing entirely for diverse groups to commit themselves to the specific practices designed to make those principles real. Everybody here, for instance, says yes to women, but not everybody here says yes to the same things for women.

Issues that brought the delegates of 180 governments around the world to Beijing for the Fourth UN Conference on Women seem almost boringly obvious now. It is 25 years since the first UN Conference on Women convened in Mexico City. The issues identified there have only gotten worse since then. The feminization of poverty, personal and public violence against women, political disenfranchisement, disempowerment and personal disregard mark the lives of women everywhere, are everywhere considered normal, even godly for women. Everywhere women are "respected," and then respectfully overlooked.

Speaker after speaker drives home the point that the time of analysis is over, that lip-service to the equality of women is not enough, that progress for women is progress for men as well. But lurking behind, masked beneath the affirmation of concern for women are other kinds of concerns as well – social, political and religious – that demand delicate negotiations in some cases and create outright conflict in others.

In the end, it is hard to know what is really being heard here: the needs of women around the world or the fears of the men who must face changes themselves in order to honor their stated resolves to respond to women in truth as well as in poetry.

The problem is not good will. The problem is that what looks essential to one part of the world often sounds threatening to another. The United States, as well as multiple other countries, for instance, is very strong in its support of reproductive rights – a position called pro-abortion by Muslim fundamentalists and Catholic groups who, in the Vatican's words, see such a move as "an attack on the family and religion." Others see the position as a necessary contribution to population control and a statement that repudiates forced sterilizations and government abortion programs in the name of one-child families, like the one in place in China itself. At the same time, the US remains very resistant to any talk of reshaping Structural Adjustment Programs in such a way that the most vulnerable members of debt-ridden societies do not bear the burden of the loss of social service programs that national governments are forced to cut in order to meet their international debt payments to the World Bank. Clearly, the living conditions of women cannot possibly change until governments release the resources to provide the kinds of services – educational, medical

and technological – that women need if they are ever to arrive at a higher standard of living in less-developed areas of the world.

Western nations, too, argue strongly that parental rights supersede the right of an underage girl to receive birth control advice, abortion information or counseling for incest independently of family guidance and consent. Many African groups, on the other hand, argue that a parental consent clause will make it impossible for girls in those areas to escape the control of fathers who use the sexual alliances of daughters to enhance their own position and will, perhaps, condemn girls to death in places where sexual involvement, particularly of daughters, constitutes a family disgrace punishable by execution.

In some areas of the world, buying, selling and trafficking in children is a heinous crime. In others, it is considered a human right for parents to dispose of their children any way they see fit.

Compromise is the major characteristic, the charism, the blessing and the bane of UN Conferences. Balancing needs, ethical considerations and religious sensibilities in an attempt to arrive at universal standards for women's rights plagues the Conference at every step. "We have come here to evangelize as well as to negotiate," Mary Ann Glendon, Chairperson of the Vatican delegation to the Conference, pointed out as her opening remark at a private meeting of NGO delegates. And, indeed, religion permeates the Conference at every turn. The Vatican is not alone in its ardor for ethical monopoly. Philosophical questions rage everywhere on this issue. Is the genital mutilation of young girls an unacceptable violation of a human being or a sacred act of religious significance? And conversely, is denouncing it a moral necessity or just one more instance of "cultural imperialism" in a multicultural world being smothered by Western standards? Is motherhood the basic definition of womanhood around which all other considerations must be constructed, or is womanhood alone the prior and determining concept to be used when defining the rights and roles of women? Is "gender" simply the consciousness that role definitions emerge out of cultural conditions and so differ from culture to culture or is it, as some critics argue, the devious ruse of depraved groups to "create another gender," the androgyne, with its destruction of macho men and female females.

The particular questions are far more difficult to separate and resolve than the agreement on overarching principles of the equality, human rights and the dignity of women. The problem is that the principles men espouse about women are just as often a smoke screen for abuse as they are a guarantee of equal rights. In too many situations, equality becomes something that women

are promised in this world but gain only in the next. Human rights becomes a code name for the civil rights that men decide to give them. Dignity, "the special nature of woman," becomes a euphemism for motherhood, unpaid work and hat-tipping. The purpose of the Beijing Platform for Action is to separate one use of principles from the other. Therefore, the Beijing Platform of Action is dangerous to the status quo in a way no statement before it has been.

Though most of the delegates to the Conference are women, most of the governments that must deal with the results of this conference are composed almost entirely of men. And therein lies the problem which underlies the problems emerging in the conference.

But all is not lost. Whatever the resolution of all the philosophical questions here, when everything is said and done three elements will measure the success of the Fourth UN Conference on Women. The first is specific attention to specific national commitments. The second is the allocation of resources to make possible the action platform adopted here. The third is gender sensitivity.

At this point, of the 109 speeches made in defense of women's rights, only 47 governments making the speeches have agreed to define specific national priorities and commitments. In addition, many countries, like the

United States, which is dealing with a Congress intent on dismantling the compassion of the country, refuse to allocate additional resources to insure that those commitments will really be kept.

But one thing remains to secure the authenticity of the Conference process. Basic to each segment of the Platform for Action is the call for "gender sensitivity," the notion that every single social action and piece of legislation in a country must first be tested for its effect on women and girls. Gender sensitivity is the measure of national sincerity that takes no money to honor and requires no commitment to specific programs over a given period of time. Gender sensitivity costs no government a penny; gender blindness costs every woman her life. That's the criteria to keep an eye on.

Gender sensitivity is the concept which, in the end, will separate national commitment from national consciousness. That's the one that unmasks lip-service to the UN Conference on Women and makes it an idea whose time has come. Will the governments of the world, our own included, and the Vatican itself, which functions in the United Nations as a city-state, critique every policy, program and allocation from the point of view of its effects on women? Or has it all been simply babbling?

Come to think about it, that's probably why the Tower of Babel did not endure. What was at issue was not language, it was truth. No one checked to see if what was being said was really real or simply double-speak, and double-speak always undermines an institution.

Fourth UN Conference on Women, Part II

The Fourth UN Conference on Women held in Beijing, China from September 4-15, 1995 is over. But it wasn't easy. Three-hundred and sixty-one paragraphs identifying twelve areas of critical concern to the role and status of women – poverty, education, health, violence, armed conflict, decision-making and public participation, structural mechanisms, gender equality, media images, universal rights, ecology and the rights of the girl-child – were finally negotiated at 5 a.m. in the morning on September 15, the very day of its ratification. The universal question, sometimes unspoken but always present at the edges of every conference conversation, however, remains: "So what?" "Who cares?" "With what effect?" The questions are well-taken: What really happened in Beijing and was it worth it?

For one thing, men can breathe a little easier now: the world has not ended. Women have not left their husbands and children. Womanhood has not been impugned. Marriage has not been rejected. Everybody leaving Beijing looks exactly the way they looked when they walked in, a little more frazzled maybe, somewhat more tired, of course, but civilized, satisfied, and well-adjusted people. Whoever the crazies are supposed to be in the Women's Movement, detractors may be disappointed to hear, they didn't come to Beijing. Housewives came, nuns came, professionals came, politicians came, social workers came. In short, the women who came to Beijing were smart, experienced, and stable. This was not a fringe group of anything. At the same time, thanks to these types, there is now something very different in the air.

Twenty years after the first UN Conference on Women, which convened in Mexico City in 1975, Beijing has repeatedly been called "historic." For the first time in history, according to Gertrude Mongella, Secretary General of the UN Fourth Conference on Women, women's issues have been recognized as societal issues, girl-children have been singled out for particular protection from sexual exploitation, and recommendations to make violence against women a criminal offense in all its forms has been accepted as necessary and just. Reality recognizes, however, that the UN can't mandate anything for anybody. So, after the dust settles and the participants go back to being teachers and mothers and delegates to nothing, will it have been worth the money, will it be seen to have merited the time, will all the paper generated by platform drafts and rewrites be justified?

There are many ways to measure those questions surely — in wages earned and public positions filled, in laws passed and quotas achieved, in terms of personal safety and human dignity and felt respect, in nutrition and education and self-determination. All those measures are sure and all of them are necessary. But all of them will take years to assess.

In the meantime, I draw my own answers to those questions from three simpler indicators: a Chinese proverb, an ominous head count, and a challenge.

In a country where the Taoist symbol for the female is water, a Chinese proverb teaches: "Water wears away the rock." For 20 years women have persistently always, even perversely at times, insisted on their rights, raised their questions and complaints, demanded to be heard over the din of male militarism and religious machoism, not simply for themselves but for the sake of women everywhere. In a world where, 20 years ago, most of the countries of the world had no idea how women spent their time, how they sustained themselves, whether or not they could read, or even how many of them there were on earth, this conference drowned in information about refugee women and old women and little girls. The invisible woman is coming into focus. The picture may not be a pretty one, by and large, but for the first time

in history, it is a real one nevertheless. For the first time in history, the human race can ask questions about women and expect to get answers.

Now, thanks to the programs designed in Beijing, women are holding the world accountable on behalf of their daughters. The Beijing Document on Women calls governments to review and modify, with the full and equal participation of women, the macro-economic and social policies which determine the world's distribution of resources.

The Platform for Action sets the year 2000 as the target date for the reduction of female illiteracy by half its 1990 level, and 2015 as the point at which the gender gap in primary and secondary school education ought to be closed.

The document leads governments to institute gender-sensitive health care, which gives priority to health programs in rural and poor urban areas.

To eliminate violence against women, the platform urges governments to condemn violence against women and to provide women with access to the mechanisms of justice which enact and enforce legislation against its perpetrators, as well as to provide shelters and support for the girls and women who are its victims.

Since women and children constitute 80% of the 23 million refugees and the 26 million displaced persons in the world, the platform calls for the inclusion of inclusion of women in national reconciliation processes and reconstruction programs and for special steps to ensure refugee and displaced women safety, civil rights and safe passage.

In most parts of the world, women are virtually absent from economic decision-making. The platform calls for the end of economic discrimination, the valuation of women's unremunerated work and equal pay for equal work.

Mechanisms for the advancement of women are called for at every level: local, regional and national.

Gender perspective is mandated in every arena.

The continued projection of negative, degrading and pornographic images of women requires balanced presentation and the access of women to the media.

The recognition that women's rights are human rights and not to be dismissed as a separate situation or a social gift of men to women requires the complete overhaul of systems and the total elimination of discrimination in all areas of human activity.

The involvement of women in environmental decision-making, the platform insists, is necessary to the preservation of the globe.

The protection of girl-children from trafficking, sexual exploitation, domestic servitude, forced labor and the abolition of all forms of discrimination and cultural oppression; the platform

states, requires national legislation and implementation.

Point: Accountability is coming to the whole human race, this time with a platform of specific priorities and clearly defined programs in hand. What Beijing began is a revolution that is more erosion than explosion. One small drop at a time, Beijing is a glimpse of the water wearing away the rock.

The second measure of the Beijing Conference lies in its sheer size. According to UN sources, attendance in Beijing doubled the attendance record of the Third UN Conference on Women in Nairobi in 1990. Over 40,000 people – delegates, representatives of Nongovernmental Organizations, and observers – came to Beijing. The Fourth UN Conference on Women was the largest international conference in the history of the world. As you read this, one thing is sure. Beijing is everywhere now. In every country of the world. In every woman's organization anywhere. In the conciousness of every government, Beijing is a Greek chorus of warnings. If the men of the world do not heed the women of the world, women will suffer, yes, but more than that, that part of the human race that is killing itself, poisoning the globe and wasting the planet will perish with them and at their own hands. The woman's question has come of age. It is not a woman's question any longer. It is the survival question of the 21st century. As a result of Beijing, feminism does not need to be apologized for any longer; it must simply be answered to. Everywhere.

Finally, the Beijing Conference on Women can be measured by the norms laid out by Gertrude Mongella, the Tanzanian Secretary-General of the Fourth UN Conference on Women. "Women," Mongella pointed out, "joined men in their struggle against slavery; women participated with men in resisting colonialism; women fought alongside men to dismantle apartheid. Now," Mongella pointed out, "men must join women in their struggle for equality."

It is time for men to stop being supportive to women in private but silent in public. It's time to see men walking alongside women for women's rights, as women walked with men in Selma and Belfast and Pietersburg and Shanghai.

We have signs of that, too. In Beijing, the Vatican emerged as a strong supporter of resource allocation for women's programs, a total life-span approach to women's health issues, supporters of family values and needs and adherents of the Cairo Document on Population Control, with its awareness of the need to promote birth control. Gone was the acrimony of the Cairo Conference and overt collusion between Vatican spokespeople and Muslim fundamentalists. In this conference, for instance, though the Vatican had reservations about the final document, rather than articulate them aloud in the plenary and be seen in cahoots with Muslim resistance, all reservations were submitted in writing to become a clear but very quiet addenda in the final publication.

At the same time, Joaquin Navarro-Valls, press secretary for the Holy See, when asked what steps the Vatican itself would take to assure women positions in decision-making roles in a church that limits authority to the clerical state, responded that the delegation, "did not speak for the 400 citizens of the Vatican but only for the 90,000,000 Catholics around the world." The Vatican, it seems, will call others to honor the needs of women but is hard put to say what it will itself do within its own confines to promote the full and equal participation of women, despite the fact that women are, in most part, missing from the decision-making processes of the church as well.

Forty Muslim countries, too, endorsed the Beijing Platform for Action but then, in the Plenary, submitted public reservations against specific items in the document — the enlarged definition of family to include more than homes with both parents present, children's rights as opposed to parental control over sexual matters, inheritance rights of female children and reproductive self-determination for women — on the grounds that these elements "violate the Shariy'eh, Islamic religious law." What governments are asked to renounce, in other words, theocratic states claim the right to maintain on theological grounds defined by men.

At the same time, 180 governments of the world have signed a document calling for programs designed to increase participation for women in decision-making bodies, give reproductive self-determination to women who are being either forcibly sterilized or impregnated against their wills, provide for the punishment of rape as war-crime, give public recognition and valuation of women's unremunerated domestic work, endorse gender sensitivity in all areas of decision-making, promise the protection of the girl-child from trafficking, early marriage and forced prostitution, enlarge economic and social roles, recognize that human rights are women's rights, and provide new access to economic resources. What's more, Beijing describes the specific programs it will take to achieve equality in all these areas.

The women along the Peace Train route who wanted economic security, personal protective legislation, health care, and political power may at least take comfort in the legitimation of their needs, whatever the remaining obstacles to their progress. After all, the Berlin Wall finally fell when least expected, ultimately the Soviet Union disintegrated, even the Great Wall of China was eventually breached. And, in case you're still inclined to doubt the persistence of change in a reactionary climate, it is important to realize that it is impossible to buy a Mao jacket and black Chinese sandals in the newly Westernized stores of China.

If Beijing proves nothing else, it may prove that change is coming for women, too, however slow the process.

Was the Fourth UN Conference on Women a success? It is a strange and decisive moment. In many instances, the statistics describing the role and status of women are getting worse every day. On the other hand, the notion that discrimination against women is moral is also getting thinner everyday as well. Maybe the Chinese are right: Maybe water really does wear away the rock.

Beyond Beijing

I spent the morning packing, feeling the sense of anti-climax too much to do much else. I had been away for six weeks, after all. Three of them on a train, three of them racing back and forth across Beijing to catch an elephant with no tail. I had been in a little capsule of a world that breathed my ideals, promised my hopes, laughed my laughs, danced my dance of life. Both worlds now seemed unreal: the one with the dream, the one without it.

When I came to Beijing I had one flight bag, one backpack and my computer. I am going home with all those things and an ungainly collapsible shopping bag to boot. Embarrassing.

The packing was finished, though, and I was far too tired to begin to write again, so quickly so we went to Bahai Park, a 12th-century prefab lake in the middle of the city, where for an hour and a half we paddled a huge fiberglass duck around a basin very much like the one in Washington, D.C. Water has always been more curative for me than anything else I can do. It didn't even bother me that most of the other boats were filled with small children. After days of agendas born out of the grief of all the women of the world, Gail and I were finally releasing a little of the child in ourselves.

Our last stop was at the oldest extant Taoist Monastery in China, where monks and nuns walked around with ivory pins through hair buns, and Buddhas of every variety looked out serenely from every meditation hall there. I smiled at the intimacy of the place and remembered that Taoism, a very feminist spirituality, had been stamped out by the powers that preferred Confucian Order to Taoist equality. I couldn't help but wonder at the end of such a conference what would win out this time. And when?

Gail's birthday is September 20th. It was as good an excuse as any to spend the night celebrating – all sorts of things. We had survived the train. I had met nine deadlines despite all the technological obstacles Eastern Europe could provide. We had gotten into China, despite the Chinese. We had traveled over 6000 miles

and then run another sixty miles a day, even when we had
stopped traveling, going from one Conference to the next. And
through it all we had not simply managed to stay on our feet for
six long weeks, we had had fun doing it.

It was a great meal and an early night with no alarm to wres-
tle with, no briefing to attend, no papers to pick up, no people to
see. There is a God.

September 17, 1995

We had a farewell coffee and chocolate torte in the airport, awash
in an overload of memories and intent on solemnizing them. If
truth were known, it was hard to leave, to go back to the struggles that attend such beliefs one person at a time. We had gotten
so used to the support of like-mindedness that there was a great
weight in the unspoken awareness that from now on we would
be back in the trenches, doing exactly what we had just done
here but one person at a time now – and alone. One person at a
time. And alone. Not surrounded by 39,000 other women to help
us.

In a quixotic last gesture to everything foreign in life, we
bought a brandy on the side and poured it into the early morning
coffee with a happy laugh. No, this was not an American breakfast, but then nothing had been for weeks. Why now?

Tiny vignettes exploded one after another in my brain. So
many things had happened in these weeks, not all of them official, but they shaped my soul just as surely as the final document
did. I remember so many little things that give texture to what
could otherwise be sterile.

- I remember Chinese soldiers in white gloves standing at the
  Conference gates, as motionless as martinets.

- I remember lunch with Betty Friedan, the grand old woman of
  the movement, who was light years ahead of its youngest
  members yet.

- I remember the feel of the board that was my bed on the train
  when I tried to roll over at night.

- I remember us buying shriveled fruits from old women and
  small trinkets from younger ones who should have been in
  offices.

- I remember the train wash basins, eight inches across, in which we all took full-size baths for weeks.

- I remember cluster after cluster of Chinese families, where three out of every four children were male, thanks to China's one-child policy, and the pain in my heart as I looked at them and heard Gail say in a low, soft voice, "Little boy, where is your sister? What did they do to your sister?"

- I remember Gertrude Mongella, soft-voiced and strong – the new image of the new Third World woman.

- I remember realizing that whites were a distinct minority at this conference, only 5000 out of over 35,000 delegates between the two conferences. This is not a white woman's agenda we're talking about here.

- I remember refusing to get out of a cab in a dark and remote section of Beijing when our country cabdriver from Huairou got lost bringing us back into the city one night. He obviously figured that the way out of his troubles was simply to put us out on the street to get a city cabdriver who did know the way. He was wrong. There was no way whatsoever that the four of us – Maria Berriozabal and Dorothy Lamm, members of the US Delegation to the UN Conference, Gail and I – were going to allow him to evict us from that cab in one of the remotest neighborhoods of Beijing. Nor were we going to pay him more money for the privilege of taking us where he had promised to take us in the first place. That cab driver became an expert on the streets of Beijing that night, and we became decidedly more assertive women. No more "darling daughter" scripts for us.

- I remember with a laugh and a slightly misty eye the wonderful little warning sign meant to measure the effect of the preservative in my fast-food sandwich. It read, "You should have eaten this four hours ago."

- I remember the perfectly manicured and balanced farm fields, each one a work of modern art, each one a study out of a Mondrian painting, each green field punctuated by one yellow tree, one red flower, one evergreen in the midst of brown haystacks. It stays in my soul as the overwhelming power of beauty and order and color to temper poverty.

- I remember the feeling of growth, of dynamism, of business bursting out of every crevice in this ancient city, and young person after young person in every crowd who is majoring in "international business."

- I remember a traffic system based on the principle that everybody should watch out for everybody else and keep going at all times.

- I remember the continuity of Chinese architecture, a city of high-rise buildings with gently sloping pagoda roofs, that signaled the continuity of the culture, the continuity of the Chinese soul across thousands of years and the promise of thousands of years to come.

Alone in the boarding area of the airport, I felt a little disorientation coming on. I had moved in a large group for so long it seemed strange to be going anywhere alone. Even community life no longer ties us into marching columns. I found myself looking around the waiting room for people I knew – and there were none. Gail was upstairs on her way to Ireland. Hundreds of other women, our life companions only yesterday, were now on their way to as many other parts of the globe as there were people there, without me. It was time for all of us to get back to something familiar. But China was China to the end. A tidal wave approaching the coast of Japan was wreaking havoc with airline schedules, one traveler told another one quietly. We waited for three hours without a single announcement or travel update. When we finally did go to the plane, that move, too, was initiated by word of mouth. I walked through the loading doors to the airplane bus on faith in humanity alone, without a clue where I would end up when I got there. It seemed a fitting finish to six weeks of total misinformation.

I have finished my final column on the Fourth UN Conference on Women in Beijing, 1995. Part of me has wings. How can anyone deny the truth, the need, the good of this? Part of me is heavy with dread. What can so few of us really do for so many against such great odds in so sinful a system?

I read in the newspaper that Frances Wood, head of the Chinese section of the British Library, now claims with reasonable certainty that Marco Polo never got to China after all. It was, she says, all a ruse. The idea gives me pause. Has the same thing happened to me? Did I only think, mistakenly think, that I had found the liberation of women in Beijing? But did we? Or was the trip only one more false start, one more cruel trick, one more wrong road, one more dead-end path in the never-ending search for the equality, humanity and development of women? The answer to those questions depends, of course, on us and what we are strong enough, brave enough to do, not simply for ourselves but for the generations of women to come.

I am someplace over who-knows-where on my way to Chicago via Anchorage, Alaska and Duluth, Minnesota. I have narrowly missed a typhoon in Japan and may miss a plane to Pittsburgh because of it. But whatever the length and meandering of the trip, I am on my way back to spend the rest of my life watching to see if anybody but me and the 40,000 other women who went to Beijing were serious about the Fourth UN Conference on Women. The daughters of our tears depend on us.